FUNDAMENTALS OF

ENGLISH GRAMMAR

Third Edition

WORKBOOK

Volume A

Betty Schrampfer Azar
with Stacy Hagen

Fundamentals of English Grammar, Third Edition
Workbook, Volume A

Copyright © 2003, 1992, 1985 by Betty Schrampfer Azar
All rights reserved.

Azar Associates
Shelley Hartle, Editor
Susan Van Etten, Manager

Pearson Education, 10 Bank Street, White Plains, NY 10606

Vice president of instructional design: Allen Ascher
Editorial manager: Pam Fishman
Project manager: Margo Grant
Development editor: Janet Johnston
Vice president, director of design and production: Rhea Banker
Director of electronic production: Aliza Greenblatt
Executive managing editor: Linda Moser
Production manager: Ray Keating
Production editor: Robert Ruvo
Director of manufacturing: Patrice Fraccio
Senior manufacturing buyer: Edie Pullman
Cover design: Monika Popowitz
Illustrations: Don Martinetti
Text composition: Carlisle Communications, Ltd.
Text font: 10.5/12 Plantin

ISBN: 0-13-013647-6

Printed in the United States of America

10 11 12 13 14 -V011- 15 14 13 12 11

Contents

PRACTICES

Chapter 3   FUTURE TIME

Chapter 4 THE PRESENT PERFECT AND THE PAST PERFECT

Chapter 5 ASKING QUESTIONS

Chapter 6   NOUNS AND PRONOUNS

Chapter 7   MODAL AUXILIARIES

PRACTICES

Preface

This ESL/EFL *Workbook* is a place for students to explore and practice English grammar on their own. It is a place where they can test and fine-tune their understandings of English structures and improve their abilities to use English meaningfully and correctly.

It is keyed to the explanatory grammar charts found in *Fundamentals of English Grammar, Third Edition,* a classroom teaching text for students of English as a second or foreign language, as well as in the accompanying *Chartbook,* a reference grammar with no exercises.

The *Workbook* is designed not only for students who desire the opportunity for independent study of English grammar but also as a resource for teachers who need exercise material for additional classwork, homework, testing, or individualized instruction.

The answers to ALL of the practices are given in the back of the book in an *Answer Key.* The *Answer Key* is on perforated pages so that it can be detached to construct a separate booklet. If teachers desire to use the *Workbook* as a classroom teaching text, the *Answer Key* can be removed at the beginning of the term.

A note on changes from the previous edition: The *Workbook* that accompanied the previous edition of *Fundamentals of English Grammar* had both self-study (answers given) and guided study (no answers given) practices. This *Workbook* has only self-study practices. The guided study practices that involved communicative, interactive, and/or task-based activities are now in the main teaching text, and other guided study practices from the previous edition have been adapted to a self-study format in this edition. A good portion of the material in this edition of the *FEG Workbook* is newly created.

CHAPTER 1
Present Time

◇ **PRACTICE 1. Interview questions and answers.**

Directions: Complete the sentences with appropriate words.

SPEAKER A: Hi. My name ____is____ Kunio.

SPEAKER B: Hi. My ____name is____ Maria. I _____ glad to meet you.

KUNIO: I _____ glad to _____ you, too. Where _____?

MARIA: I _____ from Mexico. Where _____?

KUNIO: I _____ Japan.

MARIA: Where _____ living now?

KUNIO: On Fifth Avenue in an apartment. And you?

MARIA: I _____ living in a dorm.

KUNIO: What _____ you studying?

MARIA: Business. After I study English, I'm going to attend the School of Business Administration. How _____ you? What _____ your major?

KUNIO: Engineering.

MARIA: What _____ you like to do in your free time?

KUNIO: I read a lot. How _____ you?

MARIA: I like to get on the Internet.

KUNIO: Really? What _____ you do when you're online?

MARIA: I visit many different Web sites. It _____ a good way to practice my English.

KUNIO: That's interesting. I _____ to get on the Internet, too.

MARIA: I have to _____ your full name on the board when I introduce you to the class. How _____ spell your name?

KUNIO: My first name _____ Kunio. K-U-N-I-O. My family name _____ Akiwa.

MARIA: Kunio Akiwa. _____ that right?

KUNIO: Yes, it _____. And what _____ your name again?

MARIA: My first name _____ Maria. M-A-R-I-A. My last name _____ Lopez.

KUNIO: Thanks. It's been nice talking to you.

MARIA: I enjoyed it, too.

◇ **PRACTICE 2. Present verbs. (Charts 1-1 and 1-2)**

Directions: Use the given verb to complete each sentence that follows. Use the simple present or the present progressive.

1. *sit*   I _____am sitting_____ at my desk right now.

2. *read*   I _____ the second sentence in this exercise.

3. *look*   I _____ at sentence 3 now.

4. *write*   Now I _____ the right completion for this sentence.

5. *do*   I _____ a grammar exercise.

6. *sit*   I usually _____sit_____ at my desk when I do my homework. And

   right now I _____am sitting_____ at my desk to do this exercise.

7. *read*   I often _____ the newspaper, but right now I

   _____ a sentence in my grammar workbook.

8. *look*   I _____ at the newspaper every day. But right now I

   _____ at my grammar workbook.

9. *write*   When I do exercises in this workbook, I _____ the answers in

   my book and then I check them in the *Answer Key.*★ Right now I _____

   an answer in the book.

10. *do*   I _____ grammar exercises every day. Right now I

   _____ Practice 2 in this workbook.

◇ **PRACTICE 3. Forms of the simple present. (Charts 1-1 and 1-2)**

Directions: Review the basic forms of the simple present tense by completing the sentences with the correct form of the verb ***speak***.

***PART I:* STATEMENT FORMS**

1. I *(speak)* _____speak_____ English.

2. They *(speak)* _____ English.

3. He *(speak)* _____ English.

4. You *(speak)* _____ English.

5. She *(speak)* _____ English.

***PART II:* NEGATIVE FORMS**

6. I *(speak, not)* _____do not (don't) speak_____ your language.

7. They *(speak, not)* _____ English.

8. She *(speak, not)* _____ English.

9. You *(speak, not)* _____ English.

10. He *(speak, not)* _____ English.

_____

★The *Answer Key* to these practices is in the back of this book.

11. *(you, speak)* ____Do you speak____ English?

12. *(they, speak)* _____ English?

13. *(he, speak)* _____ English?

14. *(we, speak)* _____ English?

15. *(she, speak)* _____ English?

◇ **PRACTICE 4. Forms of the present progressive. (Charts 1-1 and 1-2)**

Directions: Review the basic forms of the present progressive by completing the sentences with the correct form of the verb ***speak***.

PART I: **STATEMENT FORMS**

1. I *(speak)* ____am speaking____ English right now.

2. They *(speak)* _____ English right now.

3. She *(speak)* _____ English right now.

4. You *(speak)* _____ English right now.

5. He *(speak)* _____ English right now.

PART II: **NEGATIVE FORMS**

6. I *(speak, not)* ____am not speaking____ English right now.

7. They *(speak, not)* _____ English right now.

8. She *(speak, not)* _____ English right now.

9. You *(speak, not)* _____ English right now.

10. He *(speak, not)* _____ English right now.

PART III: **QUESTION FORMS**

11. *(you, speak)* ____Are you speaking____ English right now?

12. *(he, speak)* _____ English right now?

13. *(they, speak)* _____ English right now?

14. *(we, speak)* _____ English right now?

15. *(she, speak)* _____ English right now?

◇ **PRACTICE 5. Present verbs: questions. (Charts 1-1 and 1-2)**

Directions: Complete the questions with ***Does he*** or ***Is he***.

1. ____Is he____ a student?

2. ____Does he____ have class now?

3. _____ know his teachers?

4. _____ in the classroom?

5. _____ like school?

6. _____ a hard worker?

7. _____ tired?

8. _____ study every day?

9. _____ need help with his homework?

10. _____ studying right now?

◇ PRACTICE 6. Present verbs: questions. (Charts 1-1 and 1-2)
Directions: Complete the questions with ***Does she*** or ***Is she***.

1. ___*Is she*___ at work?

2. ___*Does she*___ work five days a week?

3. _____ working right now?

4. _____ sitting at her desk?

5. _____ come to the office every day?

6. _____ like her job?

7. _____ on the phone?

8. _____ in a meeting?

9. _____ work overtime often?

10. _____ working overtime now?

◇ PRACTICE 7. Simple present. (Charts 1-1 and 1-2)
Directions: Complete the sentences with ***do, does,*** or ***Ø***.*

1. Jack ___*does*___ not work at his father's store.

2. ___*Do*___ you have a job?

3. Kate ___*Ø*___ works at a restaurant.

4. _____ she work the day shift or night shift?

5. Denise and Scott _____ own a small company that does home repairs.

6. They _____ have different job skills.

7. They _____ not do the same work.

8. Denise _____ enjoys painting, and Scott _____ prefers woodworking.

9. Scott _____ not like painting very much.

10. They _____ get along well with each other.

11. _____ they plan to work together for a long time? Yes. They're married.

_____

*Ø = "nothing."

◇ **PRACTICE 8. Simple present and present progressive. (Charts 1-1 and 1-2)**
   Directions: Complete the sentences with **does, do, am, is, are,** or **Ø**.

   A: What _____is_____ that? What _____ you looking at?
              1   2

   B: It _____ a very rare and valuable book.
              3

   A: _____ it yours?
              4

   B: No. It _____ not belong to me. It _____ belongs to my cousin.
                   5   6

      He _____ collects old books.
              7

   A: That _____ an interesting hobby. _____ you a collector, too?
                8   9

      _____ you collect old books?
           10

   B: I _____ have the interest but not the money. Rare old books _____
            11   12

      expensive to collect. I _____ becoming interested in stamps, though. Stamps
                                  13

      _____ not as expensive as rare books. I _____ want to collect stamps from
           14   15

      the 1800s.

   A: I _____ thinking about collecting stamps, too. _____ you want to get
            16   17

      together sometime and talk about it?

   B: Yes. Let's do that.

◇ **PRACTICE 9. Simple present. (Charts 1-1 and 1-2)**
   Directions: Complete the sentences with **does, do, is, are,** or **Ø**.

   1. A turtle _____Ø_____ lays eggs.

   2. _____Do_____ snakes lay eggs?

   3. _____ an alligator lay eggs?

   4. _____ an alligator a reptile?

   5. _____ turtles and snakes reptiles?

   6. Turtles, snakes, and alligators _____

      all reptiles.

   7. Almost all reptiles _____ lay eggs.

   8. Reptiles _____ cold-blooded.

   9. They _____ prefer warm climates.

   10. Their body temperature _____ the same as the temperature of their surroundings.

   11. _____ reptiles like to lie in the sun? Yes, they do.

◇ PRACTICE 10. Simple present and present progressive. (Charts 1-1 and 1-2)
Directions: Complete the sentences with *does, do, is, are,* or *Ø*.

1. A mosquito _____is_____ flying around Sam's head.

2. Mosquitoes _____ pests.

3. They _____ bother people and animals.

4. _____ a male mosquito bite?

5. No, male mosquitoes _____ not bite.

6. Only female mosquitoes _____ bite animals and people.

7. A female mosquito _____ lays 1000 to 3000 eggs each year.

8. How long _____ mosquitoes live?

9. A female mosquito _____ lives for 30 days.

10. A male mosquito _____ not live as long as a female.

11. How long _____ a male mosquito live?

12. It _____ dies after 10 or 20 days.

13. Beverly _____ wearing mosquito repellent.

14. The mosquito repellent _____ smells bad, but it _____ works.

15. The mosquito repellent _____ effective.

16. Mosquitoes _____ stay away from people who _____ wearing mosquito repellent.

17. _____ you ever wear mosquito repellent?

18. _____ mosquito repellent work?

◇ **PRACTICE 11. Frequency adverbs. (Chart 1-3)**

Directions: Add the word in *italics* to the sentences. Put the word in its usual midsentence position.
Write Ø if no word is needed in a blank.

1. *usually*   Ann ____usually____ stays ____Ø____ at night.
2. *usually*   Ann ____Ø____ is ____usually____ at home at night.
3. *always*   Bob _____ stays _____ home in the evening.
4. *always*   He _____ is _____ at his desk in the evening.
5. *usually*   He _____ doesn't _____ go out in the evenings.
6. *always*   But he _____ doesn't _____ study every evening.
7. *sometimes*   He _____ watches _____ a little TV.
8. *never*   He _____ stays _____ up past midnight.
9. *never*   He _____ is _____ up past midnight.
10. *usually*   Does _____ Ann _____ study _____ at night?
11. *always*   Does _____ Bob _____ study _____ at night?
12. *always*   Is _____ Bob _____ at home at night?

◇ **PRACTICE 12. Frequency adverbs. (Chart 1-3)**

Directions: Add the given words to the sentence. Put the adverbs in their usual midsentence
position. Change the verb from negative to affirmative (i.e. statement form) as necessary.

1. *Sentence:* **Jane doesn't come to class on time.**

   a. *usually*   Jane ____usually doesn't come____ to class on time.
   b. *ever*   Jane ____doesn't ever come____ to class on time.
   c. *seldom*   Jane ____seldom comes____ to class on time.
   d. *sometimes*   Jane _____ to class on time.
   e. *always*   Jane _____ to class on time.
   f. *occasionally*   Jane _____ to class on time.
   g. *never*   Jane _____ to class on time.
   h. *hardly ever*   Jane _____ to class on time.

2. *Sentence:* **Jane isn't on time for class.**

   a. *usually*   Jane ____usually isn't____ on time for class.
   b. *rarely*   Jane _____ on time for class.
   c. *always*   Jane _____ on time for class.
   d. *frequently*   Jane _____ on time for class.
   e. *never*   Jane _____ on time for class.
   f. *ever*   Jane _____ on time for class.
   g. *seldom*   Jane _____ on time for class.

◇ PRACTICE 13. Frequency adverbs. (Chart 1-3)

Directions: Use the given information to complete the sentences. Use a frequency adverb for each sentence.

Kim's Day	S	M	T	W	Th	F	S
1. wake up late	X	X	X	X	X	X	X
2. skip breakfast		X	X		X		
3. visit friends	X	X		X		X	X
4. be on time for class		X	X	X	X		
5. surf the Internet				X			
6. talk on the phone	X	X	X	X		X	X
7. do homework			X			X	
8. be in bed early							

1. Kim _____always wakes_____ up late.

2. She _____ breakfast.

3. She _____ friends.

4. She _____ on time for class.

5. She _____ the Internet.

6. She _____ on the phone.

7. She _____ homework.

8. She _____ in bed early.

◇ PRACTICE 14. Frequency adverbs. (Chart 1-3)

Directions: Complete each sentence with an appropriate frequency adverb from the list.

always	*often* OR *usually*	*sometimes*
never	*seldom* OR *rarely*	

1. I watch TV in the evening five or six times a week.

   → I ___often OR usually___ watch TV in the evening.

2. I let my roommate borrow my car only one time last year.

   → I ___seldom OR rarely___ let my roommate borrow my car.

3. Maria eats cereal for breakfast seven days a week.

   → Maria _____always_____ eats cereal for breakfast.

4. Four out of five visitors to the museum stay for three hours or longer.

→ Museum visitors _____ stay for at least three hours.

5. We occasionally have quizzes in Dr. Rice's history class.

→ Dr. Rice _____ gives quizzes in her history class.

6. If the teacher is on time, the class begins at 8:00 A.M. Once in a while, the teacher is a few minutes late.

→ The class _____ begins at 8:00 A.M.

7. The train from Chicago has been late ninety percent of the time.

→ The train from Chicago is _____ on time.

8. In the desert, it rains only two or three days between May and September every year.

→ It _____ rains in the desert in the summer.

9. James asks me to go to the sailboat races every year, but I don't accept his invitation because I think sailboat racing is boring.

→ I _____ go to sailboat races with James.

10. Every time I go to a movie, I buy popcorn.

→ I _____ buy popcorn when I go to a movie.

11. Andy and Jake work in the same office and are friends. They go to lunch together four or five times a week.

→ Andy and Jake _____ go out to lunch with each other.

12. Most of the time Andy and Jake don't discuss business when they go to lunch with each other.

→ They _____ discuss business during lunch.

◇ PRACTICE 15. Frequency adverbs. (Chart 1-3)
Directions: Complete each sentence with an appropriate frequency adverb from the list and the simple present of the given verbs.

always	*often* OR *usually*	*sometimes*
never	*seldom* OR *rarely*	

1. Every time Pat rents a video, she chooses a comedy.

→ Pat *(choose)* ___**always chooses**___ a comedy to rent.

2. I almost always watch soccer matches on TV. I go to a soccer match only once a year.

→ I *(go)* _____ to a soccer match.

3. I take the bus to work once a week or once every two weeks.

→ I usually carpool to work, but I *(ride)* _____ the bus.

4. The doctor told Mari to exercise four times a week, but she works long hours and exercises only a couple of times a month.

→ Mari *(exercise)* _____ .

5. My roommate eats only vegetarian food, and I like beef and chicken. We always cook separate meals.

→ I *(eat)* _____ my roommate's meals.

6. The little boy in the street is begging for food. He comes from a poor family and never gets enough to eat.

→ The little boy *(be)* _____ hungry.

7. On most Sundays, my family gets together for a big dinner.

→ My family *(get)* _____ together for a big dinner on Sundays.

8. Usually Jane can get right to work on her computer when she turns it on, but every once in a while she gets an error message.

→ Jane *(get)* _____ an error message when she turns on her computer.

9. Peter tries to finish his homework before he goes to bed, but he usually falls asleep.

→ Peter *(finish)* _____ his homework before he falls asleep and decides to go to bed.

10. My friends like to play video games, but I don't join them because the games are too violent.

→ I *(play)* _____ video games with my friends.

11. Jenny's job starts at 8:00. Most days of the week, Jenny arrives around 7:30.

→ Jenny *(arrive)* _____ at work early.

12. I like to relax every night by taking a long, hot bath.

→ I *(take)* _____ a long, hot bath in the evening.

◇ **PRACTICE 16. Simple present: final -S/-ES. (Charts 1-4 and 1-5)**
Directions: Write *-s/-es* in the blanks where necessary. If the verb does not need *-s/-es*, use **Ø**. Change *-y* to *-i* if necessary.

1. Alan like __s__ to play soccer.

2. My son watch __es__ too much TV.

3. Rita do __es__ n't like __Ø__ coffee.

4. Monkeys climb __Ø__ trees.

5. Do _____ you like _____ to climb trees?

6. Do _____ Paul like _____ to cook?

7. Paula like _____ to dance.

8. Mike wash _____ his own clothes.

9. Yuki go _____ to school at seven.

10. Tina get _____ her work done on time.

11. Tina and Pat get _____ their work done.

12. Do _____ Bill get _____ his work done?

13. Eric do _____ n't get it done on time.

14. Ahmed carry _____ a briefcase to work.

15. Janet play _____ tennis every day.

16. A turtle is another animal that live _____ near water.

17. Bees make _____ honey.

18. A bee visit _____ many flowers in one day.

19 A frog catch _____ flies with its tongue.

20. Frogs are small green animals that live _____ near water.

◇ **PRACTICE 17. Simple present: final -S/-ES.** (Charts 1-4 and 1-5)
Directions: Read the paragraph. Then complete the paragraph about Sam's day using *he* in place of *I*. You will need to change the verbs.

SAM'S DAY:

I leave my apartment at 8:00 every morning. I walk to the bus stop and catch the 8:10 bus. It takes me downtown. Then I transfer to another bus, and it takes me to my part-time job. I arrive at work at 8:50. I stay until 1:00, and then I leave for school. I attend classes until 5:00. I usually study in the library and try to finish my homework. Then I go home around 8:00. I have a long day.

Sam _____leaves_____ his apartment at 8:00. _____He walks_____ to the bus stop and

_____ the 8:10 bus. It takes him downtown. Then _____ to

another bus, and it takes him to his part-time job. _____ at work at

8:50. _____ until 1:00, and then _____ for school.

_____ classes until 5:00. _____ usually _____ in the

library and _____ to finish his homework. Then _____ home around

8:00. _____ a long day.

◇ **PRACTICE 18. Pronunciation: final -S/-ES.** (Charts 1-5 and 6-1*)
Directions: Put the verbs under the correct endings for pronunciation.

✓cooks	stays	hates	misses
✓promises	seems	travels	draws
invites	watches	picks	introduces

/s/	/z/	/əz/
cooks		promises

_____

*See Chart 6-1, p. 157, in the Student Book for information about the pronunciation and spelling of final *-s/-es*.

◇ **PRACTICE 19. Pronunciation: final -S/-ES. (Charts 1-5 and 6-1)**
Directions: Provide the pronunciation for the verb ending: /s/, /z/, or /əz/.

1. he need/ **z** /
2. she take/ **s** /
3. the bus pass/   /
4. John love/   /
5. Pam listen/   /

6. she add/   /
7. he dress/   /
8. it fit/   /
9. the teacher enjoy/   /
10. the baby kiss/   /

11. she realize/   /
12. her dad spend/   /
13. she think/   /
14. he wonder/   /
15. my manager suggest/   /

◇ **PRACTICE 20. Spelling: final -S/-ING. (Charts 1-4, 1-5, and 2-5)**
Directions: Fill in the blanks with the simple present and present progressive forms of the verbs.

1. buy   *buys*   *is buying*
2. come   *comes*   *is coming*
3. open   _____   _____
4. begin   _____   _____
5. stop   _____   _____
6. die   _____   _____
7. rain   _____   _____
8. dream   _____   _____
9. eat   _____   _____

10. enjoy   _____   _____
11. write   _____   _____
12. try   _____   _____
13. stay   _____   _____
14. hope   _____   _____
15. study   _____   _____
16. lie   _____   _____
17. fly   _____   _____
18. sit   _____   _____

◇ **PRACTICE 21. Non-action verbs. (Chart 1-5)**
Directions: Choose the correct sentence.

1. a. We want to have an answer.
   b. We are wanting to have an answer.

2. a. The students think their grammar class is challenging.
   b. The students are thinking their grammar class is challenging.

3. a. Look! An eagle is flying overhead.
   b. Look! An eagle flies overhead.

4. a. The eagle is over there! Are you seeing it?
   b. The eagle is over there! Do you see it?

5. a. Now I believe my English is better.
   b. Now I am believing my English is better.

6. a. I'm doing this exercise now.
   b. I do this exercise now.

7. a. My parents are owning two cars at this time.
   b. My parents own two cars at this time.

8. a. This is fun. I am having a good time.
   b. This is fun. I have a good time.

9. a. We are having a new computer now.
   b. We have a new computer now.

10. a. I'm not knowing the answer to your question right now, but I'll find out.
    b. I don't know the answer to your question right now, but I'll find out.

11. a. My family is preferring chicken to red meat.
    b. My family prefers chicken to red meat.

12. a. I need to borrow some money.
    b. I am needing to borrow some money.

◇ **PRACTICE 22. Simple present and present progressive. (Charts 1-1 → 1-6)**
   Directions: Complete the sentences with the simple present or present progressive form of the verbs in the list. Each verb is used only once.

belong	need	see	✓take
bite	play	shine	understand
drive	prefer	sing	watch
look	rain	✓snow	write

1. Look outside! It _____is snowing_____. Everything is beautiful and all white.

2. My father _____takes_____ the 8:15 train into the city every weekday morning.

3. On Tuesdays and Thursdays, I walk to work for the exercise. Every Monday, Wednesday, and Friday, I _____ my car to work.

4. A: Charlie, can't you hear the telephone? Answer it!

   B: You get it! I _____ my favorite TV show. I don't want to miss anything.

5. A: What kind of tea do you like?

   B: Well, I'm drinking black tea, but I _____ green tea.

6. I'm gaining weight around my waist. These pants are too tight. I _____ a larger pair of pants.

7. A: Dinner's ready. Please call the children.

   B: Where are they?

   A: They _____ a game outside in the street.

8. It's night. There's no moon. Emily is outside. She _____ at the sky. She _____ more stars than she can count.

9. Michael has a good voice. Sometimes he _____ with a musical group in town. It's a good way to earn a little extra money.

10. A: Ouch!

   B: What's the matter?

   A: Every time I eat too fast, I _____ my tongue.

11. Nadia always _____ in her diary before bed.

12. Thank you for your help in algebra. Now I _____ that lesson.

13. This magazine is not mine. It _____ to Colette.

14. I can see a rainbow because the sun _____ and it _____

   _____ at the same time.

◇ **PRACTICE 23. Simple present and present progressive. (Charts 1-1 → 1-6)**
   Directions: Complete the sentences with the simple present or present progressive form of the verb.

   Rosa is sitting on the train right now. She *(take/not/usually)* __usually doesn't take__
   ₁
   the train, but today her son *(need)* _____ her car. She *(enjoy)*
   ₂
   _____ the ride today. There *(be)* _____ so many people
   ₃   ₄
   to watch. Some people *(eat)* _____ breakfast. Others *(drink)*
   ₅
   _____ coffee and *(read)* _____ the newspaper. One
   ₆   ₇
   woman *(work)* _____ on her laptop computer. Another *(hug)*
   ₈
   _____ her baby. Two teenagers *(play)* _____ computer
   ₉   ₁₀
   games. One of them *(wave)* _____ his hand in excitement. A clown *(walk)*
   ₁₁
   _____ up and down the aisles and *(entertain)* _____ the
   ₁₂   ₁₃
   children. Rosa *(smile)* _____ . The train ride *(take, usually)*
   ₁₄
   _____ her longer than driving, but it *(be)* _____ a more
   ₁₅   ₁₆
   enjoyable way for her to travel.

◇ **PRACTICE 24. Error analysis. (Charts 1-1 → 1-6)**
   Directions: Correct the sentences.

       1. My friend ~~don't~~ *doesn't* speak English well.

       2. I am not believing you.

       3. My sister's dog no bark.

       4. Our teacher is always starting class on time.

       5. Look! The cat gets up on the counter.

       6. Is Marie has enough money?

       7. We are not liking this rainy weather.

       8. Mrs. Gray is worry about her daughter.

       9. My brother no has enough free time.

     10. Is Jim drive to school every day?

     11. He always hurrys in the morning. He no wanting to be late.

     12. Anna have usually dinner at eight.

◇ **PRACTICE 25. Present verbs: questions and short answers. (Chart 1-7)**
   Directions: Complete the questions with *do, does, am, is,* or *are.* Then complete both the affirmative and negative short answers.

       1. A: _____ *Are* _____ you leaving now?
       B: Yes, _____ *I am* _____. OR No, _____ *I'm not* _____.

       2. A: _____ *Do* _____ your neighbors know that you are a police officer?
       B: Yes, _____ *they do* _____. OR No, _____ *they don't* _____.

       3. A: _____ you follow the same routine every morning?
       B: Yes, _____. OR No, _____.

       4. A: _____ Dr. Jarvis know the name of her new assistant yet?
       B: Yes, _____. OR No, _____.

       5. A: _____ Paul and Beth studying the problem?
       B: Yes, _____. OR No, _____.

6. A: _____ they understand the problem?

   B: Yes, _____ . OR No, _____ .

7. A: _____ Mike reading the paper and watching television at the same time?

   B: Yes, _____ . OR No, _____ .

8. A: _____ you listening to me?

   B: Yes, _____ . OR No, _____ .

9. A: _____ that building safe?

   B: Yes, _____ . OR No, _____ .

10. A: _____ you and your co-workers get together outside of work?

   B: Yes, _____ . OR No, _____ .

◇ PRACTICE 26. Review: present verbs. (Charts 1-1 → 1-7)

Directions: Use either the simple present or the present progressive of the verbs in parentheses to complete the sentences.

1. A: Hi! What *(you, do)* ___are you doing___ ?

   B: I *(watch)* _____ an exercise video. I *(want)* _____
   to lose a little weight before my vacation.

   A: I really *(enjoy)* _____ exercising. I *(go)* _____ to
   an aerobics class three times a week. It *(be)* _____ really fun. I also
   (run) _____ every morning before school.

   B: Stop! You *(make)* _____ me feel bad!

2. A: I like to read. How about you? *(you, read)* _____ a lot?

   B: Yes, I _____ . I *(read)* _____ at least one novel
   every week, and I *(subscribe)* _____ to several magazines. And I
   (look, always) _____ at the newspaper during breakfast.

3. Before you begin to study, you should ask yourself two questions. First, "Why *(I, study)*
   _____ this subject right now?" Second, "What *(I, want)* _____
   _____ to learn about this topic?" Students *(need)* _____
   to understand the purpose of their study.

4. A: I *(leave)* _____ now. *(you, want)* _____ to go
   with me into town?

   B: No, thanks. I can't. I *(wait)* _____ for my sister to call.

5. A: Shhh.

    B: Why? *(the baby, sleep)* _____ ?

    A: Uh-huh. She *(take)* _____ her afternoon nap.

    B: Okay, I'll talk softly. I *(want, not)* _____ to wake her up.

6. Ann is a painter. She *(go)* _____ to the opening of every new art show

    in the city. She *(like)* _____ to see the latest work of other artists. Right

    now she *(prepare)* _____ for a show of her new paintings next

    month.

7. It *(be)* _____ a cool autumn day today. The wind *(blow)* _____,

    _____ and the leaves *(fall)* _____ to the ground.

8. My roommate *(eat)* _____ breakfast at exactly seven o'clock every

    morning. I usually *(eat, not)* _____ breakfast at all. What time

    (you, eat) _____ in the morning?

9. A: *(you, shop)* _____ at this store every week?

    B: No, I _____ . I *(shop, usually)* _____ at the

       store near my apartment.

    A: Why *(you, shop)* _____ here now?

    B: I *(try)* _____ to find something special for my father's birthday

       dinner.

10. In cold climates, many trees *(lose)* _____ their leaves in winter. They *(rest)*

    _____ for several months. Then they *(grow)* _____

    new leaves and flowers in the spring. Some trees *(keep)* _____ their leaves

    during the winter and *(stay)* _____ green all year long. In some regions of

    the earth, trees *(grow, not)* _____ at all. For example, some desert areas

    (have, not) _____ any trees. The largest area of the world without trees

    (be) _____ Antarctica. No trees *(grow)* _____ in

    Antarctica.

CHAPTER 2
Past Time

◇ **PRACTICE 1. Simple past. (Charts 2-1 → 2-7)**

Directions: Change the sentences to past time. Use simple past verbs and ***yesterday*** or ***last***.

PRESENT	PAST
every day	*yesterday*
every morning	*yesterday morning*
every afternoon	*yesterday afternoon*
every night	*last night*
every week	*last week*
every Monday, Tuesday, etc.	*last Monday, Tuesday, etc.*
every month	*last month*
every year	*last year*

1. I **walk** to my office **every morning**.

   → I ____walked____ to my office ____yesterday____ **morning**.

2. I **talk** to my parents on the phone **every week**.

   → I ____talked____ to my parents on the phone ____last____ **week**.

3. The post office **opens** at eight o'clock **every morning**.

   → The post office _____ at eight o'clock _____ **morning**.

4. Mrs. Hall **goes** to the fruit market **every Monday**.

   → Mrs. Hall _____ to the fresh fruit market _____ **Monday**.

5. The company managers **meet** at nine o'clock **every Friday morning**.

   → The executives _____ at nine o'clock _____ **Friday morning**.

6. I **make** my own lunch and **take** it to work with me **every morning**.

   → _____ **morning**, I _____ my own lunch and _____ it to work with me.

7. Mr. Clark **pays** his rent on time **every month**.

→ Mr. Clark _____ his rent on time _____ **month**.

8. The baby **falls** asleep at three o'clock **every afternoon**.

→ _____ **afternoon**, the baby _____ asleep at three o'clock.

9. The last bus to downtown **leaves** at ten o'clock **every night**.

→ The last bus to downtown _____ at ten o'clock _____ **night**.

◇ PRACTICE 2. Simple past: regular and irregular verbs. (Charts 2-2 and 2-7)
Directions: Write the simple past form of the given verbs.

1. start	_started_		16. bring	_____
2. go	_went_		17. break	_____
3. see	_____		18. eat	_____
4. stand	_____		19. watch	_____
5. arrive	_____		20. build	_____
6. win	_____		21. take	_____
7. have	_____		22. pay	_____
8. make	_____		23. leave	_____
9. finish	_____		24. wear	_____
10. feel	_____		25. open	_____
11. fall	_____		26. decide	_____
12. hear	_____		27. plan	_____
13. sing	_____		28. write	_____
14. explore	_____		29. teach	_____
15. ask	_____		30. hold	_____

◇ PRACTICE 3. Simple past forms. (Charts 2-1 → 2-3)
Directions: Use the given words to create questions and answers.

1. *you/answer*

A: The teacher asked a question. ____Did you answer____ it?

B: Yes, ____I did____ . ____I answered____ it. OR

No, ____I didn't____ . ____I didn't answer____ it.

2. *he/see*

    A: Tom went to the celebration. _____ the fireworks?

    B: Yes, _____ . _____ the fireworks. OR

        No, _____ . _____ the fireworks.

3. *they/watch*

    A: The game was on TV. _____ it?

    B: Yes, _____ . _____ the game. OR

        No, _____ . _____ the game.

4. *you/understand*

    A: You went to a lecture. _____ it?

    B: Yes, _____ . _____ the lecture. OR

        No, _____ . _____ the lecture.

5. *you/be*

    A: _____ at home last night?

    B: Yes, _____ . _____ at home last night. OR

        No, _____ . _____ at home last night.

◇ **PRACTICE 4. Present and past negatives. (Chapter 1 and Charts 2-1 → 2-3)**

Directions: The sentences in quotation marks contain incorrect information. Complete the unfinished sentences by using correct information: first in a negative sentence, then in an affirmative sentence.

1. "You flew to school yesterday."

    No, I ___didn't fly___ to school yesterday. I ___walked/took the bus___ .

2. "Lemons are sweet."

    No, lemons _____ sweet. They _____ .

3. "Astronauts walked on Mars in 1969."

    No, astronauts _____ on Mars in 1969. They _____

    in 1969.

4. "You were a baby in the year 2000."

    No, I _____ in 2000. I _____ years old in 2000.

5. "Buddha came from China."

    No, Buddha _____ from China. Buddha _____

    from Nepal.

6. "Coffee comes from cocoa beans."

No, coffee _____ from cocoa beans. It _____ .

7. "You slept outdoors last night."

No, I _____ outdoors last night. I _____ .

8. "Ice is hot."

No, ice _____ hot. It _____ .

9. "Dinosaurs disappeared a hundred years ago."

No, dinosaurs _____ a hundred years ago.

They _____ ago.

◇ PRACTICE 5. Simple past: questions. (Charts 2-2 and 2-3)
Directions: Write past tense questions using the italicized words and *did, was,* or *were*.

1. *he/study*   ___Did he study___ yesterday?

2. *he/sick*   ___Was he sick___ yesterday?

3. *she/sad*   _____ yesterday?

4. *they/eat*   _____ yesterday?

5. *they/hungry*   _____ yesterday?

6. *you/go*   _____ yesterday?

7. *she/understand* _____ yesterday?

8. *he/forget*   _____ yesterday?

◇ PRACTICE 6. Simple past: questions. (Charts 2-2 and 2-3)
Directions: You took your driver's test yesterday. A friend is asking you questions about it. Fill in the blanks with *did, was,* or *were*.

1. ___Did___ you pass your driver's test yesterday?

2. _____ you nervous?

3. _____ your hands shake?

4. _____ you practice a lot for it?

5. _____ the license examiner friendly?

6. _____ you make any silly mistakes?

7. _____ the car easy to drive?

8. _____ you go on an easy route?

◇ **PRACTICE 7. Simple past: regular and irregular verbs. (Charts 2-2 and 2-7)**

Directions: Complete the sentences by using the simple past of the verbs below. Use each verb only once.

call	hold	sell	swim
fight	jump	✓shake	teach
freeze	ride	stay	think

1. Paul _____shook_____ the soft drink so hard that it sprayed all over his clothes.

2. Carol didn't want to go on vacation with us, so she _____ home alone all week.

3. Since I hurt my knee, I can't go jogging. Yesterday, I _____ in the pool for an hour instead.

4. I was terrified just standing over the pool on the high diving board. Finally, I took a deep breath, held my nose, and _____ into the water.

5. The climber, who was fearful of falling, _____ the rope tightly in both hands.

6. Johnny pushed Alan down on the floor, and the two boys _____ for a few minutes. Neither boy was hurt.

7. Before Louise started her own company, she _____ chemistry at the university.

8. It was extremely cold last night, and the water we put out for the cat _____ solid.

9. Before I made my decision, I _____ about it for a long, long time.

10. Carlos _____ your house three times to ask you to go to the movie with us, but there was no answer, so we went without you.

11. My car wouldn't start this morning, so I _____ my bicycle to work.

12. I needed money to pay my tuition at the university, so I _____ my motorcycle to my cousin.

◇ **PRACTICE 8. Regular verbs: pronunciation of -ED endings. (Chart 2-4)**
Directions: Practice pronouncing final *-ed* by saying the words in the list aloud.

1. stopped = stop/t/
2. robbed = rob/d/
3. wanted = want/əd/
4. talked = talk/t/
5. lived = live/d/
6. needed = need/əd/
7. passed = pass/t/*
8. pushed = push/t/
9. watched = watch/t/
10. thanked = thank/t/

11. finished = finish/t/
12. seem = seem/d/
13. killed = kill/d/
14. turned = turn/d/
15. played = play/d/
16. continued = continue/d/
17. repeated = repeat/əd/
18. waited = wait/əd/
19. added = add/əd/
20. decide = decide/əd/

◇ **PRACTICE 9. Regular verbs: pronunciation of -ED endings. (Chart 2-4)**
Directions: Write the correct pronunciation. Then practice pronouncing final *-ed* by saying the words in the list aloud.

1. talked = talk/ t /
2. lived = live/ d /
3. waited = wait/ əd /
4. played = play/   /
5. added = add/   /
6. needed = need/   /
7. killed = kill/   /
8. finished = finish/   /
9. seemed = seem/   /
10. repeated = repeat/   /

11. continued = continue/   /
12. watched = watch/   /
13. passed = pass/   /
14. decide = decide/   /
15. stopped = stop/   /
16. turned = turn/   /
17. thanked = thank/   /
18. wanted = want/   /
19. robbed = rob/   /
20. pushed = push/   /

◇ **PRACTICE 10. Spelling and pronunciation of -ED endings. (Charts 2-4 and 2-5)**
Directions: Add *-ed* to each verb. When necessary, add or change letters to correct the spelling. Then circle the correct pronunciation of *-ed* for the given verb.

1. walk_ed_____ (/t/) /d/ /əd/
2. pat_ted_____ /t/ /d/ (/əd/)
3. worry_ied_____ /t/ (/d/) /əd/
4. stay_____ /t/ /d/ /əd/
5. visit_____ /t/ /d/ /əd/
6. die_____ /t/ /d/ /əd/
7. trade_____ /t/ /d/ /əd/
8. plan_____ /t/ /d/ /əd/

9. open_____ /t/ /d/ /əd/
10. hurry_____ /t/ /d/ /əd/
11. rent_____ /t/ /d/ /əd/
12. try_____ /t/ /d/ /əd/
13. enjoy_____ /t/ /d/ /əd/
14. stop_____ /t/ /d/ /əd/
15. need_____ /t/ /d/ /əd/

---

*The words "passed" and "past" have the same pronunciation.

◇ PRACTICE 11. Regular verbs: pronunciation of -ED endings. (Chart 2-4)
Directions: Practice pronouncing final **-ed** by reading the sentences aloud.

1. I **watched** TV. Jean **listened** to the radio. Nick **waited** for the mail.
   watch/t/   listen/d/   wait/əd/

2. I **tasted** the soup. It **seemed** too salty.
   taste/əd/   seem/d/

3. James **planned** for his future. He **saved** money and **started** his own business.
   plan/d/   save/d/   start/əd/

4. I **asked** a question. Joe **answered** it. Then he **repeated** the answer for Ted.
   ask/t/   answer/d/   repeat/əd/

5. I **stared** at the sculpture for a long time. Finally, I **touched** it.
   stare/d/   touch/t/

6. Mary **prepared** a long report for her boss. She **completed** it late last night.
   prepare/d/   complete/əd/

7. After Dick **parked** the car, I **jumped** out and **opened** the door for my mother.
   park/t/   jump/t/   open/d/

8. After I **finished** reading Rod's poem, I **called** him and we **talked** for an hour.
   finish/t/   call/d/   talk/t/

9. Earlier today, I **cleaned** my apartment.
   clean/d/

10. I **washed** the windows, **waxed** the wood floor, and **vacuumed** the carpet.
    wash/t/   wax/t/   vacuum/d/

11. I **crossed** my fingers and **hoped** for good news.
    cross/t/   hope/t/

◇ PRACTICE 12. Spelling of -ING and -ED forms. (Chart 2-5)
Directions: Complete the chart. Refer to Chart 2-5 if necessary.

END OF VERB	DOUBLE THE CONSONANT?	SIMPLE FORM	-ING	-ED
-e	NO	excite	*exciting*	*excited*
Two Consonants		*exist*		
Two Vowels + One Consonant		*shout*		
One Vowel + One Consonant		ONE-SYLLABLE VERBS *pat*		
		TWO-SYLLABLE VERBS (STRESS ON **FIRST** SYLLABLE) *visit*		
		TWO-SYLLABLE VERBS (STRESS ON **SECOND** SYLLABLE) *admit*		
-y		*pray* *pry*		
-ie		*tie*		

◇ **PRACTICE 13. Spelling of -ING. (Chart 2-5)**

Directions: Add *-ing* to the verbs and write them in the correct columns.

1. hit	4. take	7. learn	10. smile	13. begin
2. come	5. hop	8. listen	11. stay	14. win
3. cut	6. hope	9. rain	12. study	15. write

Double the consonant. (stop → stopping)	Drop the -e. (live → living)	Just add -ing. (visit → visiting)
hitting		

◇ **PRACTICE 14. Spelling of -ING and -ED. (Chart 2-5)**

Directions: Spell the *-ing* and *-ed* forms of the verbs. (The simple past/past participle of irregular verbs is given in parentheses.)

	-ING	-ED
1. ride	riding	(ridden)
2. start	starting	started
3. come		(came)
4. happen		
5. try		
6. buy		(bought)
7. hope		
8. keep		(kept)
9. tip		
10. fail		
11. fill		
12. feel		(felt)
13. dine		
14. mean		(meant)
15. win		(won)
16. learn		
17. listen		
18. begin		(began)

◇ **PRACTICE 15. Spelling of -ING. (Chart 2-5)**

Directions: Write one "t" or two "t"s in the blanks to spell the *-ing* verb form correctly. Then write the simple form of the verb in each sentence.

SIMPLE FORM

1. I'm wai t___ ing for a phone call.   1. ___wait___

2. I'm pe tt ing my dog.   2. ___pet___

3. I'm bi ____ ing my nails because I'm nervous.   3. _____

4. I'm si ____ ing in a comfortable chair.   4. _____

5. I'm wri ____ ing in my book.   5. _____

6. I'm figh ____ the urge to have some ice cream.   6. _____

7. I'm wai ____ ing to see if I'm really hungry.   7. _____

8. I'm ge ____ ing up from my chair now.   8. _____

9. I'm star ____ ing to walk to the refrigerator.   9. _____

10. I'm permi ____ ing myself to have some ice cream.   10. _____

11. I'm lif ____ ing the spoon to my mouth.   11. _____

12. I'm ea ____ ing the ice cream now.   12. _____

13. I'm tas ____ ing it. It tastes good.   13. _____

14. I'm also cu ____ ing a piece of cake.   14. _____

15. I'm mee ____ ing my sister at the airport tomorrow.   15. _____

16. She's visi ____ ing me for a few days. I'll save some   16. _____

    cake and ice cream for her.

◇ PRACTICE 16. Spelling of irregular verbs. (Chart 2-7)
Directions: The given verbs are in the present tense. Write the past tense of these verbs.

PART I.

buy   b <u>o</u> <u>u</u> g <u>h</u> t

bring   br __ __ __ __ t

teach   t __ __ __ __ t

catch   c __ __ __ __ t

fight   f __ __ __ __ t

think   th __ __ __ __ t

find   f __ __ __ d

PART II.

swim   sw __ __

drink   dr __ __ __

sing   s __ __ __

ring   r __ __ __

PART III.

blow   bl __ __

draw   dr __ __

fly   fl __ __

grow   gr __ __

know   kn __ __

throw   thr __ __

PART IV.

break   br __ __ __

write   wr __ __ __

freeze   fr __ __ __

ride   r __ __ __

sell   s __ __ __

steal   st __ __ __

PART V.

hit   h __ __

hurt   h __ __ __

read   r __ __ __

shut   sh __ __

cost   c __ __ __

put   p __ __

quit   q __ __ __

PART VI.

pay   p __ __ d*

say   s __ __ d*

---

*The pronunciations of *paid* and *said* are different.
    Paid rhymes with *made.*
    Said rhymes with *red.*

◇ **PRACTICE 17. Irregular verbs. (Chart 2-7)**

Directions: Complete the sentences with the simple past of the given irregular verbs. There may be more than one possible completion.

begin	*drive*	*hurt*	*ring*	*think*
build	*eat*	*keep*	*rise*	*write*
come	*fall*	*lead*	*shut*	
do	*freeze*	*pay*	*steal*	
drink	*have*	*run*	*take*	

1. Sue _____*drank/had*_____ a cup of coffee before class this morning.

2. We _____ a delicious dinner at a Mexican restaurant last night.

3. When it _____ to rain yesterday afternoon, I _____ all of the windows in the apartment.

4. The phone _____ eight times before anybody answered it.

5. My brother and his wife _____ to our apartment for dinner last night.

6. The architectural firm that I work for designed that building. My brother's construction company _____ it. They took two years to complete it.

7. When Alan slipped on the icy sidewalk yesterday, he _____ down and _____ his back. His back is very painful today.

8. Alice called the police yesterday because someone _____ her bicycle while she was in the library studying. She's very angry.

9. There was a cool breeze last night. I opened the window, but Colette got cold and _____ it.

10. Ted _____ his car across Canada last summer.

11. Rita _____ faster than anyone else in the footrace.

12. None of the other runners was ever in front of Rita during the race. She _____ all of the other runners in the race from start to finish.

13. Greg is very cheap. I was surprised when he _____ for my dinner.

14. It was really cold yesterday. The temperature was three below zero.* I nearly _____ to death when I walked home!

_____

*Note: -3°F (Fahrenheit) equals -20°C (Centigrade or Celsius).

15. Jason _____ an excellent job in gluing the broken vase together.

16. The sun _____ at 6:21 this morning.

17. I _____ about going to Florida for my vacation, but I finally decided to go to Puerto Rico.

18. My friend _____ a note and passed it to me in class.

19. My mother _____ all the letters I wrote to her while I was in England. She didn't throw any away.

20. An earthquake destroyed the old bridge, so the town _____ a new one across the river.

◇ **PRACTICE 18. Irregular verbs. (Chart 2-7)**
Directions: Complete the sentences with the simple past of any of the given irregular verbs. There may be more than one possible completion.

break	draw	give	quit	steal
buy	fall	grow	read	teach
choose	feel	hear	shake	
cut	find	lose	sleep	
dig	forget	meet	speak	

1. A: Why isn't Bill here for the meeting? He's supposed to give the weekly report.
   B: I ____spoke____ to him on the phone last night, and he said he'd be here.

2. After I gave a large bone to each of my three dogs, they went to separate corners of the backyard and _____ holes to bury their bones.

3. After looking at all the chairs, I finally _____ the red one. It was a difficult decision.

4. The players are depressed because they _____ the game last weekend. Next time they'll play better.

5. A: How can you take a three-month vacation? What about your job?
   B: I won't be going back to that job ever again. I _____ yesterday.

6. Laurie has circles under her eyes because she _____ only two hours last night. She was studying for her final exams.

7. Matt lost his watch. He looked everywhere for it. Finally, he _____ it in his pants that were in the washing machine. He had washed his watch, but it was still ticking.

8. Joy was barefoot. She stepped on a piece of broken glass and _____ her foot.

9. Danny and I are old friends. We _____ each other in 1985.

10. My father _____ me how to make furniture.

11. The student with the highest grade point average _____ a speech at the graduation ceremony. She _____ about her hopes for the future of the world.

12. I didn't have a garden, so I _____ tomatoes in a pot on the balcony outside my apartment.

13. Paul was in a hurry to get to class this morning. He _____ to comb his hair.

14. Last week I _____ an interesting book about the volcanoes in Iceland.

15. When Erica and I were introduced to each other, we _____ hands.

16. Mike is in jail because he _____ a car.

17. When I heard about Sue's problem, I _____ sorry for her.

18. The students all _____ pictures of their teacher, but few of the drawings looked like her. She tried not to laugh at the pictures.

19. A few minutes ago, I _____ on the radio about a bad plane accident.

20. Joe had an accident. He _____ off the roof and _____ his leg.

◇ PRACTICE 19. Review: past questions and negatives. (Charts 2-1 → 2-3)
Directions: Rewrite the subjects and verbs that appear in boldface to create questions and negative statements. Omit the rest of each sentence.

	QUESTION	NEGATIVE
1. **I rode** a bus.	Did I ride	I didn't ride
2. **She sat** down.		
3. **We were** on time.		
4. **They tried** hard.		

5. **He was** late. _____ _____

6. **They cut** some paper. _____ _____

7. **She threw** a ball. _____ _____

8. **We did** our work. _____ _____

◇ **PRACTICE 20. Simple present and past: questions.** (Chapter 1, Charts 2-1 → 2-5, and preview of Chapter 5)

Directions: Create questions using the SIMPLE PAST or the SIMPLE PRESENT.

SITUATION: Your cousin, Susan, has a new friend. She was with her new friend last night. You have several questions.

1. *what/do last night?*

   A: ____What did you do last night?____
   B: I went to a concert with my new friend.

2. *what/your friend's name?*

   A: ____What is your friend's name?____
   B: Robert.

3. *he/nice?*

   A: _____
   B: Yes, he's very nice.

4. *how/your evening?*

   A: _____
   B: Fine.

5. *where/you/go?*

   A: _____
   B: To a concert.

6. *you/enjoy it?*

   A: _____
   B: Very much.

7. *the music/loud?*

   A: _____
   B: Yes, very loud! I loved it.

8. *what time/you/get home?*

   A: _____
   B: Around midnight.

9. *what/you/wear?*

   A: _____
   B: Nothing special. Just some jeans and a sweater.

10. *what/he/be like?*
    (his personality)

    A: _____
    B: He's funny and friendly. He's really nice.

11. *what/he/look like?*

    A: _____
    B: He has dark hair and is medium height.

12. *you/want to go out with him again?*

    A: _____
    B: Yes. I like him a lot.

◇ PRACTICE 21. Review: simple present, present progressive, and simple past forms. (Chapter 1 and Charts 2-1 → 2-7)

Directions: Complete the chart with the correct forms of the verbs.

EVERY DAY	NOW	YESTERDAY
1. He **is** here every day.	He ___is___ here now.	He ___was___ here yesterday.
2. I _think_ about you every day.	**I'm thinking** about you now.	I ___thought___ about you yesterday.
3. We **play** tennis every day.	We _____ tennis now.	We _____ tennis yesterday.
4. I _____ juice every day.	I _____ juice now.	**I drank** juice yesterday.
5. He _____ every day.	He **is teaching** now.	He _____ yesterday.
6. She _____ every day.	She _____ now.	She **swam** yesterday.
7. You **sleep** late every day.	You _____ now.	You _____ late yesterday.
8. He _____ every day.	He **is reading** now.	He _____ yesterday.
9. They _____ hard every day.	They _____ hard now.	They **tried** hard yesterday.
10. We **eat** dinner every day.	We _____ dinner now.	We _____ dinner yesterday.

◇ PRACTICE 22. Simple present and simple past. (Chapter 1 and Charts 2-1 → 2-7)

Directions: Use the simple present or the simple past form of the verb in parentheses as appropriate. Complete the short answers to the questions.

1. A: *(you, hear)* ___Did you hear___ the thunder last night?

   B: No, I ___didn't___ . I *(hear, not)* ___didn't hear___ anything all night. I *(be)* ___was___ asleep.

2. A: Listen! *(you, hear)* ___Do you hear___ a siren in the distance?

   B: No, I ___don't___ . I *(hear, not)* ___don't hear___ anything at all.

3. A: That's a nice bookshelf. *(you, build)* _____ it?

   B: No, I _____ . My uncle *(build)* _____ it for me.

4. A: I have a question. *(a fish, be)* _____ slippery to hold?

   B: Yes, _____ . It can slip right out of your hand.

   A: How about frogs? *(they, be)* _____ slippery?

   B: Yes, _____ .

   A: What about snakes?

   B: I *(know, not)* _____ . I've never touched a snake.

5. A: I *(want)* _____ to go to the mall later this afternoon and look for a new

   bathing suit. *(you, want)* _____ to go with me?

   B: I can't. I *(have)* _____ an appointment with my English teacher. Besides,

   I *(buy)* _____ a new bathing suit last year. I *(need, not)* _____

   _____ a new one this year.

6. I always *(offer)* _____ to help my older neighbor carry her groceries into her

   house every time I see her return from the store. She *(be)* _____ always very

   grateful. Yesterday, she *(offer)* _____ to pay me for helping her, but of

   course I *(accept, not)* _____ the offer.

7. Last Monday night, I *(take)* _____ my sister and her husband to my favorite

   restaurant for dinner and *(find)* _____ the doors locked. I *(know, not)*

   _____ it then, but the restaurant *(be, not)* _____ open on

   Mondays. We *(want, not)* _____ to eat anywhere else, so we *(go)*

   _____ back to my house. I *(make)* _____ a salad and *(heat)*

   _____ some soup. Everyone *(seem)* _____ satisfied even

   though I *(be, not)* _____ a wonderful cook.

8. My daughter is twenty-one years old. She *(like)* _____ to travel. My wife and

   I *(worry)* _____ about her a little when she *(be)* _____ away from

   home, but we also *(trust)* _____ her judgment.

   Last year, after she *(graduate)* _____ from college, she *(go)*

   _____ to Europe with two of her friends. They *(travel, not)* _____

   _____ by train or by car. Instead, they *(rent)* _____

   motor scooters and *(ride)* _____ slowly through each country they visited.

   While she *(be)* _____ away, my wife and I *(worry)* _____

   about her safety. We *(be)* _____ very happy when we *(see)* _____ her

   smiling face at the airport and *(know)* _____ that she was finally safe at home.

◇ PRACTICE 23. Past progressive. (Charts 2-8 and 2-9)

Directions: Complete the sentences by using the past progressive of the given verbs. Use each verb only once.

✓hide	look	read	sing	sit	talk	watch

1. Jack's wife arranged a surprise birthday party for him. When Jack arrived home, several people _____were hiding_____ behind the couch or behind doors. All of the lights were out, and when Jack turned them on, everyone shouted "Surprise!"

2. The birds began to sing when the sun rose at 6:30. Dan woke up at 6:45. When Dan woke up, the birds _____ .

3. I _____ a video last night when my best friend called.

4. While we _____ on the phone, the power went out.

5. The bus driver looked at all the passengers on her bus and noticed how quiet they were. Some people _____ newspapers or books. Most of the people _____ quietly in their seats and _____ out the windows of the bus.

◇ PRACTICE 24. Past progressive. (Charts 2-8 and 2-9)

Directions: Complete the sentences. Use the simple past for one clause and the past progressive for the other.

ACTIVITY IN PROGRESS	NADIA	GEORGE	BILL
play soccer	break her glasses	score a goal	hurt his foot
hike	find some money	see a bear	pick up a snake
dance	trip and fall	meet his future wife	get dizzy

1. While Nadia _____was playing_____ soccer, she _____broke_____ her glasses.

2. George _____scored_____ a goal while he _____was playing_____ soccer.

3. Bill _____ his foot while he _____ soccer.

4. While Nadia _____ , she _____ some money.

5. George _____ a bear while he _____ .

6. Bill _____ a snake while he _____ .

7. Nadia _____ and _____ while she _____ .

8. While George _____ , he _____ his future wife.

9. While Bill _____ , he _____ dizzy.

◇ **PRACTICE 25. Past progressive vs. simple past. (Charts 2-8 and 2-9)**

Directions: Complete the sentences with the verbs in parentheses. Use the simple past or the past progressive.

1. It *(begin)* _____began_____ to rain while Amanda and I *(walk)*

    _____were walking_____ to school this morning.

2. While I *(wash)* _____ dishes last night, I *(drop)*

    _____ a plate and *(break)* _____ it.

3. I *(see)* _____ Ted at the student cafeteria at lunchtime yesterday. He *(eat)*

    _____ a sandwich and *(talk)* _____ with some

    friends. I *(join)* _____ them.

4. While I *(walk)* _____ under an apple tree a few days ago, an apple

    (fall) _____ and *(hit)* _____ me on the head.

5. Robert didn't answer the phone when Sara called. He *(sing)* _____

    his favorite song in the shower and *(hear, not)* _____ the phone ring.

6. A: I saw a whale!

    B: Really? Great! When?

    A: This morning. I *(walk)* _____ on the beach when I *(hear)*

    _____ a sudden "whoosh!" It *(be)* _____ the spout of

    a huge gray whale.

7. A: There was a power outage in our part of town last night. *(your lights, go out)* _____

    _____ too?

    B: Yes, they did. It *(be)* _____ terrible! I *(take)* _____ a

    shower when the lights went out. My wife *(find)* _____ a flashlight and

    rescued me from the bathroom. We couldn't cook dinner, so we *(eat)* _____

    sandwiches instead. I *(try)*

    _____ to read some

    reports by candlelight, but I couldn't

    see well enough, so I *(go)*

    _____ to bed

    and *(sleep)* _____ .

    How about you?

8. Yesterday Tom and Janice *(go)* _____ to the zoo, where they *(see)*

_____ many kinds of animals and *(have)* _____ a few

adventures. While they *(walk)* _____ by an elephant, it *(begin)*

_____ to squirt water at them, so they run behind a rock and *(dry)*

_____ themselves. Later, while they *(pass)* _____

the giraffe area, one of the tall, purple-tongued animals *(lower)* _____ its

head toward Tom and *(start)* _____ to nibble on his green hat. Janice

said, "Shoo!"* At that point, the giraffe *(stretch)* _____ its head toward

Janice and *(try)* _____ to eat her ice cream cone. Janice *(let, not)*

_____ the giraffe have the ice cream because she *(stand)*

_____ right in front of a sign that said, "DO NOT FEED THE

ANIMALS." She *(point)* _____ at the sign and *(say)* _____

to the giraffe, "Can't you read?"

◇ **PRACTICE 26. Past time using time clauses. (Chart 2-10)**
Directions: Combine the two sentences in any order, using the time expression in parentheses.
Underline the time clause.

1. I gave Alan his allowance. He finished his chores. *(after)*
   → *I gave Alan his allowance <u>after he finished his chores.</u>* OR
   → *<u>After Alan finished his chores,</u> I gave him his allowance.*

2. The doorbell rang. I was climbing the stairs. *(while)*

3. The firefighters checked the ashes one last time. They went home. *(before)*

4. The Novaks stopped by our table at the restaurant. They showed us their new baby. *(when)*

5. We started to dance. The music began. *(as soon as)*

6. We stayed in our seats. The game ended. *(until)*

7. My father was listening to a baseball game on the radio. He was watching a basketball game

   on television. *(while)*

---

*"Shoo! Shoo!" means "Go away! Leave!" When the woman *shooed* the giraffe, that means she said "Shoo! Shoo!" and made
the giraffe leave.

◇ PRACTICE 27. Past verbs. (Charts 2-1 → 2-10)
Directions: Complete the sentences with the correct form of the verbs in parentheses.

Last Friday was a holiday. It (be) _____ Independence Day, so I didn't
                                           1
have to go to classes. I (sleep) _____ a little later than usual. Around ten, my
                                         2
friend Larry (come) _____ over to my apartment. We (pack) _____
                            3   4
a picnic basket and then (take) _____ the bus to Forest Park. We (spend)
                                          5
_____ most of the day there.
         6

When we (get) _____ to the park, we (find) _____ an empty
                         7   8
picnic table near a pond. There were some ducks on the pond, so we (feed) _____
                                                                                              9
them. We (throw) _____ small pieces of bread on the water, and the ducks
                          10

(swim) _____ over to get them. One duck was very clever. It (catch)
                 11
_____ the bread in midair before it (hit) _____ the water.
         12   13
Another duck was a thief. It (steal) _____ bread from the beaks of other ducks.
                                             14
While we (feed) _____ the ducks, Larry and I (meet) _____
                         15   16
a man who usually (come) _____ to the park every day to feed the ducks. We
                                 17
(sit) _____ on a park bench and (speak) _____ to him for fifteen
          18   19
or twenty minutes.

After we (eat) _____ our lunch, I
_____ 20

(take) _____ a short nap under a tree.
_____ 21

While I (sleep) _____ , a
_____ 22

mosquito (bite) _____ my arm. When I
_____ 23

(wake) _____ up, my arm itched, so I
_____ 24

scratched it. Suddenly I (hear) _____ a
_____ 25

noise in the tree above me. I (look) _____
_____ 26

up and (see) _____ an orange and gray
_____ 27

bird. After a few moments, it (fly) _____
_____ 28

away.

During the afternoon, we (do) _____ many things. First we (take)
_____ 29

_____ a long walk. When we (get) _____ back to our picnic table,
_____ 30 _____ 31

I (read) _____ a book, and Larry, who (be) _____ an artist,
_____ 32 _____ 33

(draw) _____ pictures. Later we (play) _____ a game of chess.
_____ 34 _____ 35

Larry (win) _____ the first game, but I (win) _____ the second
_____ 36 _____ 37

one. Then he (teach) _____ me how to play a new game, one with dice. While
_____ 38

we (play) _____ , one of the dice (fall) _____ from the
_____ 39 _____ 40

picnic table onto the ground. We finally (find) _____ it in some tall grass.
_____ 41

In the evening, we (join) _____ a huge crowd to watch the fireworks display.
_____ 42

The fireworks (be) _____ beautiful. Some of the explosions (be) _____
_____ 43 _____ 44

very loud, however. They *(hurt)* _____ my ears. When the display *(be)*

_____ over, we *(leave)* _____ . All in all, it *(be)* _____

a very enjoyable day.

◇ **PRACTICE 28. Past habit with USED TO. (Chart 2-11)**
   Directions: Using the given information, complete the sentences. Use ***used to***.

   1. When James was young, he hated school. Now he likes school.

      → James _____used to hate school_____ .

   2. Ann was a secretary for many years, but now she owns her own business.

      → Ann _____ , but now she owns her own business.

   3. Rebecca had a pet rat when she was ten. The rat died, and she hasn't had another rat as a pet
      since that time.

      → Rebecca _____ as a pet.

   4. Before Adam got married, he went bowling five times a week.

      → Adam _____ five times a week.

   5. When we raised our own chickens, we had fresh eggs every morning.

      → We _____ every morning when we raised

      our own chickens.

   6. When Ben was a child, he often crawled under his bed and put his hands over his ears when
      he heard thunder.

      → Ben _____ and

      _____ when he heard thunder.

7. When I lived in my home town, I went to the beach every weekend. Now I don't go to the beach every weekend.

   → I _____ to the beach every weekend, but now I don't.

8. Adam has a new job. He has to wear a suit every day. When he was a student, he always wore jeans.

   → Adam _____ a suit every day, but now he does.

9. Sara has two cats that she enjoys as pets. In the past, she hated cats. These are her first pets.

   → Sara _____ cats. She _____

   pets, but today she enjoys her two cats.

10. Now you have a job every summer. Have you always worked during summers?

   → What _____ in summer?

◇ PRACTICE 29. Error analysis. (Chapter 2)
Directions: Correct the errors.

1. They ~~don't stayed~~ *didn't stay* at the park very long last Saturday.

2. They are walked to school yesterday.

3. I was understand all the teacher's questions yesterday.

4. We didn't knew what to do when the fire alarm ringed yesterday.

5. I was really enjoyed the baseball game last week.

6. Mr. Rice didn't died in the accident.

7. I use to live with my parents. but now I have my own apartment.

8. My friends were went on vacation together last month.

9. I didn't afraid of anything when I am a child.

10. The teacher was changed his mind yesterday.

11. Sally love Jim, but he didn't loved her.

12. Carmen no used to eat fish, but now she does.

◇ **PRACTICE 30. Past verbs. (Chapter 2)**

Directions: Complete the sentences with the simple past or the past progressive of the verbs in parentheses.

Late yesterday afternoon while I *(prepare)* _____was preparing_____ dinner, the doorbell
                                                        1

(ring) _____ . I *(put)* _____ everything down and *(rush)*
                    2   3

_____ to answer it. I *(open)* _____ the door and *(find)*
            4   5

_____ a delivery man standing in my doorway. He *(hold)*
            6

_____ an express mail package and *(need)* _____ me to sign
            7   8

for it. While I *(deal)* _____ with the delivery man, the phone *(ring)*
                                9

_____ . I *(excuse)* _____ myself and *(reach)* _____
            10   11   12

for the phone. While I *(try)* _____ to talk on the phone and sign for the
                                        13

package at the same time, my young son *(run)* _____ up to me to tell me about
                                                        14

the cat. The cat *(try)* _____ to catch a big fish in my husband's prized
                            15

aquarium. The fish *(swim)* _____ frantically to avoid the cat's paw.
                                    16

I *(say)* _____ an abrupt goodbye to the telemarketer on the phone and
            17

(hang) _____ up. I *(thank)* _____ the delivery man and *(shut)*
          18   19

_____ the door. I *(yell)* _____ at the cat and *(shoo)*
       20   21

_____ her away from the fish. Then I *(sit)* _____ down in an easy
       22   23

chair and *(stay)* _____ there until I *(begin)* _____ to feel calm
                      24   25

again. But as soon as I *(feel)* _____ like everything was under control, the
                                      26

doorbell *(ring)* _____ again. Then the phone *(ring)* _____ . Then
                     27   28

my son said, "Mom! Mom! The dog is in the refrigerator!" I couldn't move. "What's next?" I

said aloud to no one in particular.

CHAPTER 3
Future Time

◇ **PRACTICE 1. Present, past, and future. (Chapters 1, 2, and 3)**
Directions: Complete the sentences with the given verbs. Use the simple present, the simple past, and *be going to/will*.

1. *arrive*   a. Joe ___arrives___ on time **every day.**

    b. Joe ___arrived___ on time **yesterday.**

    c. Joe ___is going to arrive___ on time **tomorrow.**   OR

    Joe ___will arrive___ on time **tomorrow.**

2. *eat*   a. Ann _____ breakfast **every day.**

    b. Ann _____ breakfast **yesterday.**

    c. Ann _____ breakfast **tomorrow.**   OR

    Ann _____ breakfast **tomorrow.**

3. *arrive, not*   a. Mike _____ on time **every day.**

    b. Mike _____ on time **yesterday.**

    c. Mike ___isn't going to arrive___ on time **tomorrow.**   OR

    Mike _____ on time **tomorrow.**

4. *eat?*   a. _____ you _____ breakfast **every day?**

    b. _____ you _____ breakfast **yesterday?**

    c. _____ you _____ breakfast **tomorrow?**   OR

    _____ you _____ breakfast **tomorrow?**

5. *eat, not*   a. I _____ breakfast **every day.**

    b. I _____ breakfast **yesterday.**

    c. I _____ breakfast **tomorrow.**   OR

    I _____ breakfast **tomorrow**

◇ PRACTICE 2. WILL and BE GOING TO. (Charts 3-1 → 3-3)
   Directions: Complete the chart with the correct forms of the verbs.

be going to		will	
I ___am going to___ leave.		I ___will___ leave.	
You _____ leave.		You _____ leave.	
Mr. Rose _____ leave.		He _____ leave.	
We _____ leave.		We _____ leave.	
Our parents _____ leave.		They _____ leave.	
The boys (not) _____ leave.		They (not) _____ leave.	
Ann (not) _____ leave.		She (not) _____ leave.	
I (not) _____ leave.		I (not) _____ leave.	

◇ PRACTICE 3. BE GOING TO. (Chart 3-2)
   Directions: Complete the sentences by using a pronoun + a form of **be going to**.

1. I ate lunch with Alan today, and ___I'm going to eat___ lunch with him tomorrow too.

2. Jason wasn't in class today, and ___he isn't going to be___ in class tomorrow either.

3. The students took a quiz yesterday, and _____ another quiz today.

4. Margaret walked to school this morning, and _____ to school tomorrow morning too.

5. It isn't raining today, and according to the weather report, _____ tomorrow either.

6. We're in class today, and _____ in class tomorrow too.

7. You didn't hitchhike to school today, and _____ to school tomorrow either.

8. I didn't get married last year, and _____ married this year either.

9. Peter didn't wear a clean shirt today, and _____ a clean one tomorrow either.

◇ PRACTICE 4. WILL. (Chart 3-3)
   Directions: Read the paragraph. Change all the verbs with **be going to** to **will**.

                     will

The Smiths ~~are going to~~ celebrate their 50th wedding anniversary on December 1 of this

year. Their children are planning a party for them at a local hotel. Their family and friends are

going to join them for the celebration.

Mr. and Mrs. Smith have three children and five grandchildren. The Smiths know that two of their children are going to be at the party, but the third child, their youngest daughter, is far away in Africa, where she is doing medical research. They believe she is not going to come home for the party.

The Smiths don't know it, but their youngest daughter is going to be at the party. She is planning to surprise them. It is going to be a wonderful surprise for them! They are going to be very happy to see her. The whole family is going to enjoy being together for this special occasion.

◇ **PRACTICE 5. Questions with WILL and BE GOING TO. (Charts 3-1 → 3-3)**
Directions: Use the given information to complete the questions. Write the question forms for both *will* and *be going to*.

1. Nick is thinking about *starting* an Internet company. His friends are wondering:

   _____Will Nick start_____ an Internet company?

   _____Is Nick going to start_____ an Internet company?

2. The teacher, Mr. Jones, is thinking about *giving* a test. His students are wondering:

   _____ a test?

   _____ a test?

3. Jacob is thinking about *quitting* his job. His co-workers are wondering:

   _____ his job?

   _____ his job?

4. Mr. and Mrs. Kono are thinking about *adopting* a child. Their friends are wondering:

   _____ a child?

   _____ a child?

5. The Johnsons are thinking about *moving*. Their friends are wondering:

   _____?

   _____?

6. Dr. Johnson is thinking about *retiring*. Her patients are wondering:

   _____?

   _____?

◇ PRACTICE 6. WILL. (Chart 3-3)
   Directions: Complete the dialogues. Use ***will.***

1. A: *(you, help)* ___Will you help___ me tomorrow?
   B: Yes, ___I will*___ .   OR   No, ___I won't___ .

2. A: *(Paul, lend)* _____ us some money?
   B: Yes, _____ .   OR   No, _____ .

3. A: *(Jane, graduate)* _____ this spring?
   B: Yes, _____ .   OR   No, _____ .

4. A: *(her parents, be)* _____ at the ceremony?
   B: Yes, _____ .   OR   No, _____ .

5. A: *(I, benefit)* _____ from this business deal?
   B: Yes, _____ .   OR   No, _____ .

◇ PRACTICE 7. WILL PROBABLY. (Chart 3-4)
   Directions: Complete the sentences with ***will*** or ***won't.*** Also use ***probably.***

1. The clouds are leaving, and the sun is coming out. It ___probably won't___ rain anymore.

2. The weather is cold today. There's no reason to expect the weather to change. It ___will probably___ be cold tomorrow too.

3. Sam, Sharon, and Carl worked hard on this project. They _____ turn in the best work. The other students didn't work as hard.

4. Ronald is having a very difficult time in advanced algebra. He didn't understand anything that happened in class today, and he _____ understand tomorrow's class either.

5. Jan skipped lunch today. She _____ eat as soon as she gets home.

6. I don't like parties. Mike really wants me to come to his birthday party, but I _____ _____ go. I'd rather stay home.

---

*Pronouns are NOT contracted with helping verbs in short answers.
   CORRECT: *Yes, I will.*   INCORRECT: *Yes, I'll.*

7. Conditions in the factory have been very bad for a long time. All of the people who work on the assembly line are angry. They _____ vote to go out on strike.

8. We are using up the earth's resources at a rapid rate. We _____ continue to do so* for years to come.

◇ **PRACTICE 8. WILL PROBABLY. (Chart 3-4)**
Directions: Complete the sentences.

PART I. Use a pronoun + **will/won't**. Use **probably**.
1. I went to the library last night, and ____I'll probably go____ there tonight too.

2. Ann didn't come to class today, and ____she probably won't come____ tomorrow either.

3. Greg went to bed early last night, and _____ to bed early tonight too.

4. Jack didn't hand his homework in today, and _____ it in tomorrow either.

5. The students had a quiz today, and _____ one tomorrow too.

PART II. Use a pronoun + **be going to/not be going to**. Use **probably**.
6. I watched TV last night, and ____I'm probably going to watch____ TV tonight too.

7. I wasn't at home last night, and _____ at home tonight either.

8. It's hot today, and _____ hot tomorrow too.

9. My friends didn't come over last night, and _____ over tonight either.

10. Alice didn't ride her bike to school today, and _____ it to school tomorrow either.

◇ **PRACTICE 9. Sureness about the future. (Chart 3-4)**
Directions: Decide if the speaker is 100%, 90%, or 50% sure.

1. __90%__ You'll probably hear from our office tomorrow.

2. _____ Gino may not finish his assignment on time.

3. _____ My roommate will transfer to another university next year.

_____

*Do so means "do that thing I just talked about." In this sentence, *do so* = *use up the earth's resources at a rapid rate.*

4. _____ My roommate is probably going to change her major.

5. _____ Julia may join a health club next month.

6. _____ I will probably join a health club too.

7. _____ Karen and Lee are not going to continue dating each other.

8. _____ Maybe they will remain friends.

◇ **PRACTICE 10. Sureness about the future. (Chart 3-4)**

Directions: Answer each question by using the word in parentheses. Pay special attention to word order.

1. A: Are Joel and Rita going to have a simple wedding? *(probably)*

   B: Yes. Joel and Rita _____*are probably going to have*_____ a simple wedding.

2. A: Are they going to invite a lot of people? *(probably not)*

   B: No. They _____

   a lot of people.

3. A: Will they get married in Rita's garden? Or will they get married at a place of worship?
   (may, maybe)

   B: They're not sure. They _____ in Rita's garden.

   _____ they _____ at a place of worship.

4. A: Is Rita going to rent her wedding dress? *(may)*

   B: She's trying to save money, so she's thinking about it. She _____ her
   wedding dress.

5. A: Will she decide that she wants a wedding dress of her very own? *(probably)*

   B: She _____ that she wants a wedding dress of her very own.

6. A: Will Joel feel very relaxed on his wedding day? Will he be nervous? *(may not, may)*

   B: Joel _____ very relaxed on his wedding day. He _____

   _____ a little nervous.

7. A: Are they going to go on a honeymoon? *(will)*

   B: Yes. They _____ on a honeymoon immediately after the

   wedding, but they haven't told anyone where they are going to go.

8. A: Will they go far away for their honeymoon? *(probably not)*

   B: They _____ far. They have only a few days before

   they need to be back at work.

◇ **PRACTICE 11. WILL. (Chart 3-5)**
   Directions: Complete the dialogues with ***will*** and a verb from the list. Use each verb only once.

✓ answer	hold	move	take
get	leave	read	turn off

1. At the office: A: The phone's ringing.
                         B: I _'ll answer it_____.

2. At home: A: The baby won't stop crying.
                         B: I _____ her.

3. At the doctor's   A: I feel hot.
   office: B: I _____ your temperature.

4. At work: A: These boxes are in the way.
                         B: I _____ them.

5. At home: A: The oven's still on.
                         B: I _____ it _____.

6. At a restaurant: A: You paid the bill. I _____ the tip.
                         B: Thanks!

7. At home: A: The mail's here.
                         B: I _____ it.

8. At a fast-food   A: I don't have my glasses. I can't read the menu board.
   restaurant: B: I _____ it to you.

◇ **PRACTICE 12. BE GOING TO vs. WILL. (Chart 3-5)**
   Directions: Complete the sentences with either ***be going to*** or ***will***.*

1. *(Speaker B is planning to listen to the news at six.)*

   A: Why did you turn on the radio?

   B: I _'m going to_____ listen to the news at six.

2. *(Speaker B didn't have a plan to show the other person how to solve the math problem, but she is happy to do it.)*

   A: I can't figure out this math problem. Do you know how to do it?

   B: Yes. Give me your pencil. I _'ll_____ show you how to solve it.

_____

*Usually ***be going to*** and ***will*** are interchangeable: you can use either one of them with little difference in meaning. Sometimes, however, they are NOT interchangeable. In this exercise, only one of them is correct, not both. See Chart 3-5, p. 63, in the *FEG 3e* student book.

3. *(Speaker B has made a plan. He is planning to lie down because he doesn't feel well.)*

   A: What's the matter?

   B: I don't feel well. I _____ lie down for a little while. If anyone calls, tell them I'll call back later.

   A: Okay. I hope you feel better.

4. *(Speaker B did not plan to take the other person home. He volunteers to do so only after the other person talks about missing his bus.)*

   A: Oh no! I wasn't watching the time. I missed my bus.

   B: That's okay. I _____ give you a ride home.

   A: Hey, thanks!

5. *(Speaker B already has a plan.)*

   A: Why did you borrow money from the bank?

   B: I _____ buy a new pickup.* I've already picked it out.

6. *(Speaker B does not have a plan.)*

   A: Mom, can I have a candy bar?

   B: No, but I _____ buy an apple for you. How does that sound?

   A: Okay, I guess.

7. *(Speaker B has already made her plans about what to wear. Then Speaker B volunteers to help.)*

   A: I can't figure out what to wear to the dance tonight. It's informal, isn't it?

   B: Yes. I _____ wear a pair of nice jeans.

   A: Maybe I should wear my jeans, too. But I think they're dirty.

   B: I _____ wash them for you. I'm planning to do a load of laundry in a few minutes.

   A: Gee, thanks. That'll help me out a lot.

◇ **PRACTICE 13. BE GOING TO vs. WILL. (Chart 3-5)**
   Directions: Complete the sentences with either *be going to* or *will*.

   1. A: Can I borrow this book?

      B: Sure. But I need it back soon.

      A: I __'ll_____ return it to you tomorrow. Okay?

   2. A: I __'m going to_____ wear a dark suit to the wedding reception. How about you?

      B: I'm not sure.

   3. A: What are you doing with that picture?

      B: It doesn't look good in this room. I _____ hang it in our bedroom.

———————
*A *pickup* is a small truck.

4. A: Can you meet me for dinner after work?

   B: I'd like to, but I can't. I _____ work late tonight.

5. A: It's grandfather's eighty-fifth birthday next Sunday. What _____

   you _____ give him for his birthday?

   B: I _____ give him a walking stick that I made myself.

6. A: Gee, I'd really like an ice cream cone, but I didn't bring any money with me.

   B: That's okay. I _____ buy one for you.

   A: Thanks!

7. A: Why are you looking for a screwdriver?   SCREW

   B: One of the kitchen chairs has a loose screw. I _____

   _____ fix it.

8. A: The computer printer isn't working again! What am I going to do?

   B: Calm down. Give Tom a call. He _____

   fix it for you. He just fixed my printer.   SCREWDRIVER

9. A: Why is Nadia going to leave work early today?

   B: She _____ pick up her husband at the airport.

10. A: Achoo! Your cat is making me sneeze.

    B: I _____ put her outside.

    A: Thanks.

11. A: Do you have any plans for Saturday?

    B: I _____ help some friends move to their new home.

12. A: Your pants have ink on them.

    B: They do? I don't have another pair.

    A: Don't worry. I have some spot remover. I _____ get it for you.

◇ **PRACTICE 14. Past and future time clauses. (Charts 2-10 and 3-6)**
    Directions: Underline the time clauses.

1. <u>After I did my homework last night,</u> I went to bed.

2. I'm going to go to bed <u>after I do my homework tonight</u>.

3. Before Bob left for work this morning, he locked the door.

4. Before Bob leaves for work this morning, he's going to lock the door.

5. I'll call you after I get home this evening.

6. I called my friend after I got home last night.

7. Class will begin as soon as the teacher arrives.

8. As soon as the teacher arrived, class began.

9. When the rain stops, we'll go for a walk.

10. We went for a walk when the rain stopped.

◇ **PRACTICE 15. Future time clauses. (Chart 3-6)**
    Directions: Combine the ideas of the two given sentences into one sentence by using a time clause.
    Use the word in parentheses to introduce the time clause.

1. *First:*   I'm going to finish my homework.
   Then: I'm going to go to bed.
   (after)   ____<u>After I finish</u>____ my homework, ____<u>I'm going to go</u>____ to bed.

2. *First:*   I'll finish my homework.
   Then: I'm going to go to bed.
   (until)   ____<u>I'm not going to go</u>____ to bed ____<u>until I finish</u>____ my homework.

3. *First:*   Ann will finish her homework.
   Then: She will watch TV tonight.*
   (before)   _____ TV tonight, _____ her
                homework.

4. *First:*   Jim will get home tonight.
   Then: He's going to read the newspaper.
   (after)   _____ the newspaper _____
                home tonight.

5. *First:*   I'll call John tomorrow.
   Then: I'll ask him to my party.
   (when)   _____ John tomorrow, _____ him
                to my party.

_____

*A noun usually comes before a pronoun:
        *After **Ann** eats dinner, **she** is going to study.*
        ***Ann** is going to study after **she** eats dinner.*

6. *First:*   Mrs. Fox will stay in her office tonight.
   Then: She will finish her report.

   (until)   _____ in her office tonight _____

   _____ her report.

7. *First:*   I will get home tonight.
   Then: I'm going to take a hot bath.

   (as soon as)   _____ home tonight, _____

   a hot bath.

8. *First:*   I'm going to be in Bangkok.
   Then: I'm going to go to a Thai-style boxing match.

   (while)   _____ in Bangkok, _____ to a

   Thai-style boxing match.

◇ PRACTICE 16. IF-clauses. (Chart 3-6)

   Directions: Using the given ideas, complete each sentence by using an *if*-clause. Use a comma if necessary.*

   1. Maybe it will rain tomorrow.

      _____**If it rains tomorrow,**_____ I'm going to go to a movie.

   2. Maybe it will be hot tomorrow.

      _____ I'm going to go swimming.

   3. Maybe Adam will have enough time.

      Adam will finish his essay tonight _____.

   4. Maybe I won't get a check tomorrow.

      _____ I'll e-mail my parents.

   5. Perhaps the weather will be nice tomorrow.

      We're going to go on a hike _____.

   6. Maybe Gina won't study for her test.

      _____ she'll get a bad grade.

   7. Maybe I will have enough money.

      I'm going to go to Hawaii for my vacation _____.

   8. Maybe I won't study tonight.

      _____ I probably won't pass the chemistry exam.

   _____

   *Notice the punctuation in the example. A comma is used when the *if*-clause comes before the main clause. No comma is used when the *if*-clause follows the main clause.

◇ PRACTICE 17. Time clauses and IF-clauses. (Chart 3-6)

Directions: Combine the ideas in the two sentences into one sentence by using the word in *italics* to make an adverb clause. Omit the words in parentheses from your new sentence. <u>Underline</u> the adverb clause.

1. *when*   a. I'll see you Sunday afternoon.
                b. I'll give you my answer (then).*

       → <u>When I see you Sunday afternoon,</u> I'll give you my answer. OR
         I'll give you my answer <u>when I see you Sunday afternoon.</u>

2. *before*   a. I'm going to clean up my apartment (first).
                b. My friends are going to come over (later).

3. *when*   a. The storm will be over (in an hour or two).
                b. I'm going to do some errands (then).

4. *if*   a. (Maybe) you won't learn how to use a computer.
                b. (As a result), you will have trouble finding a job.

5. *as soon as*   a. Joe will meet us at the coffee shop.
                b. He'll finish his report (soon).

6. *after*   a. Sue will wash and dry the dishes.
                b. (Then) she will put them away.

7. *if*   a. They may not leave at seven.
                b. (As a result), they won't get to the theater on time.

◇ PRACTICE 18. Review: past and future. (Chapters 2 and 3)

Directions: Read Part I. Use the information in Part I to complete Part II with appropriate verb tenses. Use **will** (not **be going to**) for future time in Part II. Use the simple present for present time.

PART I.

(1) Yesterday morning was an ordinary morning. I got up at 6:30. I washed my face and brushed my teeth. Then I put on my jeans and a sweater. I went to the kitchen and started the electric coffee maker.

---

*When you combine the sentences, omit the word in parentheses.

(2) Then I walked down my driveway to get the morning newspaper. While I was walking to get the paper, I saw a deer. It was eating the flowers in my garden. After I watched the deer for a little while, I made some noise to make the deer run away before it destroyed my flowers.

(3) As soon as I got back to the kitchen, I poured myself a cup of coffee and opened the morning paper. While I was reading the paper, my teenage daughter came downstairs. We talked about her plans for the day. I helped her with her breakfast and made a lunch for her to take to school. After we said goodbye, I ate some fruit and cereal and finished reading the paper.

(4) Then I went to my office. My office is in my home. My office has a desk, a computer, a radio, a fax, a copy machine, and a lot of bookshelves. I worked all morning. While I was working, the phone rang many times. I talked to many people. At 11:30, I went to the kitchen and made a sandwich for lunch. As I said, it was an ordinary morning.

PART II.

(1) Tomorrow morning ___will be___ an ordinary morning. I ___'ll get___ up at 6:30. I ___'ll wash___ my face and ___brush___ my teeth. Then I _____ probably _____ on my jeans and a sweater. I _____ to the kitchen and _____ the electric coffee maker.

(2) Then I _____ down my driveway to get the morning newspaper. If I _____ a deer in my garden, I _____ it for a while and then _____ some noise to chase it away before it _____ my flowers.

(3) As soon as I _____ back to the kitchen, I _____ myself a cup of coffee and _____ the morning paper. While I'm reading the paper, my teenage daughter _____ downstairs. We _____ about her plans for the day. I _____ her with her breakfast and _____ a lunch for her to take to school. After we _____ goodbye, I _____ some fruit and cereal and _____ reading the paper.

(4) Then I _____ to my office. My office _____ in my home. My office _____ a desk, a computer, a radio, a fax, a copy machine, and a lot of bookshelves. I _____ all morning. While I'm working, the phone _____ many times. I _____ to many people. At 11:30, I _____ to the kitchen and _____ a sandwich for lunch. As I said, it _____ an ordinary morning.

◇ PRACTICE 19. Using BE GOING TO and the present progressive to express future time. (Chart 3-7)

Directions: Rewrite the sentences by using **be going to** and the present progressive.

1. I'm planning to stay home tonight.

   _____I'm going to stay_____ home tonight.

   _____I'm staying_____ home tonight.

2. They're planning to travel across the country by train this summer.

   _____ across the country by train this summer.

   _____ across the country by train this summer.

3. We're planning to get married in June.

   _____ married in June.

   _____ married in June.

4. He's planning to start graduate school next year.

   _____ graduate school next year.

   _____ graduate school next year.

5. She's planning to go to New Zealand next month.

   _____ to New Zealand next month.

   _____ to New Zealand next month.

6. My neighbors are planning to build their dream home this spring.

   _____ their dream home this spring.

   _____ their dream home this spring.

◇ PRACTICE 20. Using the present progressive to express future time. (Chart 3-7)

Directions: Complete the sentences with the present progressive. Use each verb in the list only once. Notice the future time expressions in *italics*.

arrive	*come*	*meet*	*see*	*take*
attend	*get*	*plan*	*speak*	✓*travel*
call	*leave*	*prepare*	*study*	

1. Kathy _____is traveling_____ to Caracas *next month* to attend a conference.

2. A: Your apartment is so neat! Are you expecting guests?

   B: Yes. My parents _____ *tomorrow* for a two-day visit.

3. A: Do you have any plans for lunch today?

   B: I _____ Shannon at the Shamrock Cafe *in an hour.* Want to join us?

4. A: I _____ a bicycle for my son for his birthday *next month.* Do you know anything about bikes for kids?

   B: Sure. What do you want to know?

5. Amanda likes to take her two children with her on trips whenever she can, but she _____ not _____ them with her to El Paso, Texas, *next week.* It's strictly a business trip.

6. A: What are your plans for the rest of the year?

   B: I _____ French in Grenoble, France, *this coming summer.* Then I'll be back here in school in the fall.

7. A: Why are you packing your suitcase?

   B: I _____ for Los Angeles *in a couple of hours.*

8. My regular dentist, Dr. Jordan, _____ a conference in Las Vegas *next week,* so I _____ her partner, Dr. Peterson, when I go in for my appointment *next Friday.*

9. A: Do we have a test in English class tomorrow?

   B: No. Don't you remember? We're going to have a guest lecturer.

   A: Really? Who? Are you sure we don't have a test?

   B: A professor from the Department of Environmental Sciences _____ to our class tomorrow morning.

   A: Great! That sounds interesting. And it's a lot better than having a test.

10. A: My sister and her husband _____ over to my house for dinner tomorrow night. It's my sister's birthday, so I _____ a special birthday dinner for her. I _____ her favorite food: roast beef and mashed potatoes.

    B: That's nice. She'll like that.

11. A: I'm going to call the doctor. You have a fever, chills, and a stomach ache.

    B: No, don't call a doctor. I'll be okay.

    A: I'm worried. I _____ the doctor! And that's it!

◇ **PRACTICE 21. Using the simple present to express future time. (Chart 3-8)**

Directions: Use any of the verbs in the list to complete the sentences. Use the simple present to express future time.

arrive	*depart*	*get in*	*open*
begin	*end*	*land*	*start*
close	*finish*	*leave*	

1. A: What time ____does____ class ____begin/start____ tomorrow morning?

   B: It ____begins/starts____ at eight o'clock sharp.

2. A: The coffee shop _____ at seven o'clock tomorrow morning. I'll meet you

   there at 7:15.

   B: Okay. I'll be there.

3. A: What time are you going to go to the airport tonight?

   B: Tom's plane _____ around 7:15, but I think I'll go a little early in case it

   gets in ahead of schedule.

4. A: What's the hurry?

   B: I've got to take a shower, change clothes, and get to the theater fast. The play

   _____ in forty-five minutes, and I don't want to miss the beginning.

5. A: What time _____ the dry cleaning shop _____ this evening?

   If I don't get there in time, I'll have nothing to wear to the banquet tonight.

   B: It _____ at 6:00. I can pick up your dry cleaning for you.

   A: Hey, thanks! That'll really help!

6. A: What time should we go to the theater tomorrow night?

   B: The doors _____ at 6:00 P.M., but we don't need

   to be there that early. The show _____ at 8:00.

   If we _____ at the theater by 7:15, we'll be there

   in plenty of time. The show _____ around 10:30,

   so we can be back home by a little after 11:00.

7. A: I've enjoyed my visit with you, but tomorrow I have to go back home.

   A: What time _____ your flight _____ tomorrow?

   B: It _____ at 12:34 P.M. I want to be at the airport an hour early, so we

   should leave here around 10:30, if that's okay with you.

   A: Sure. What time _____ your flight _____ in Mexico City?

   B: It's about a three-hour flight. I'll get in around 4:30 Mexico City time.

◇ PRACTICE 22. Using BE ABOUT TO. (Chart 3-9)
   Directions: Write sentences using ***be about to***. Use each verb in the list only once.

| break | leave | ✓rain | ring | write |

1. A: What does it usually mean if the sky is cloudy and dark?

   B: It usually means that it ____is about to rain____ .

2. A: What does it probably mean if Jack is standing by the front door with his car keys in his hand?

   B: It means that he _____ the house.

3. A: What does it mean if the teacher picks up a piece of chalk?

   B: It probably means that she _____ on the board.

4. A: You're in the kitchen. The oven timer has only a few seconds left. What does that mean?

   B: The timer _____ .

5. A: The heavy snow is making the tree branches hang down. One is almost touching the ground. What's going to happen?

   B: The branch _____ probably

      _____ .

◇ PRACTICE 23. Parallel verbs. (Chart 3-10)
   Directions: Complete the sentences with the verbs in parentheses.

1. My classmates are going to meet at Danny's and *(study)* ____study____ together tonight.

2. Tomorrow the sun will rise at 6:34 and *(set)* _____ at 8:59.

3. Last night, I was listening to music and *(do)* _____ my homework when Kim stopped by.

4. Next weekend, Nick is going to meet his friends downtown and *(go)* _____ to a soccer game.

5. My pen slipped out of my hand and *(fall)* _____ to the floor.

6. Alex is at his computer. He *(write)* _____ e-mails and *(wait)* _____ for responses.

7. Every morning without exception, Mrs. Carter *(take)* _____ her dog for a walk and *(buy)* _____ a newspaper at Charlie's newsstand.

8. Before I *(go)* _____ to your boss and *(tell)* _____ her about your mistake, I want to give you an opportunity to explain it to her yourself.

9. Next month, I *(take)* _____ my vacation and *(forget)* _____ about everything that is connected to my job.

10. Kathy thinks I was the cause of her problems, but I wasn't. Someday she *(discover)* _____ the truth and *(apologize)* _____ to me.

◇ **PRACTICE 24. Error analysis. (Chapter 3)**
Directions: Correct the errors.

1. My friends will ~~to~~ join us after work.

2. Maybe the rain stops soon.

3. On Friday, our school close early so teachers can go to a workshop.

4. My husband and I will intend to be at your graduation.

5. Our company is going to sells computer equipment to schools.

6. Give grandpa a hug. He's about to leaving.

7. Mr. Scott is going to retire and moving to a warmer climate.

8. If your soccer team will win the championship tomorrow, we'll have a big celebration for you.

9. I maybe won't be able to meet you for coffee.

10. I bought this cloth because I will make some curtains for my bedroom.

11. I moving to London when I will finish my education here.

12. Are you going go to the meeting?

13. I opened the door and walk to the front of the room.

14. When will you be going to move into your new apartment?

Directions: Complete the sentences by using a form of the words in parentheses.

1. It's getting late, but before I *(go)* _____go_____ to bed, I *(finish)* _____
_____ my homework and *(write)* _____ a couple of e-mails.

2. While I *(make)* _____ dinner last night, some grease *(spill)*
_____ out of the frying pan and *(catch)* _____ on
fire. When the smoke detector on the ceiling *(start)* _____ to buzz, my
roommate *(run)* _____ into the kitchen to find out what was wrong. He
(think) _____ that the house was on fire!

3. Mark is obsessed with video games. He *(play)* _____ video games morning,
noon, and night. Sometimes he *(cut)* _____ class to play them. Right now he
(do, not) _____ very well in
school. If he *(study, not)* _____
_____ harder and *(go)*
_____ to class every day, he *(flunk)*
_____ out of school.

4. Sometimes my daughter, Susie, has temper
tantrums. She *(cry)* _____ and
(stomp) _____ her feet when she
(get) _____ angry. Yesterday when
she *(get)* _____ angry, she *(pick)* _____ up a toy car and
(throw) _____ it at her little brother. Luckily, the car *(hit, not)* _____
_____ him. Susie *(feel)* _____ very bad. She *(apologize)*
_____ to her brother and *(kiss)* _____ him.

5. It's October now. The weather *(begin)* _____ to get colder. It *(begin)*
_____ to get cold every October. I *(like, not)* _____
winter, but I *(think)* _____ autumn is beautiful. In a couple of weeks, my
friend and I *(take)* _____ a weekend trip to the country if the
weather *(be)* _____ nice. We *(drive)* _____ through the
river valley and *(enjoy)* _____ the colors of fall.

6. Jane *(meet)* _____ me at the airport when my plane *(arrive)* _____ tomorrow.

7. If I *(see)* _____ Mike tomorrow, I *(tell)* _____ him about the party.

8. I go to New York often. When I *(be)* _____ in New York, I usually *(see)* _____ a Broadway play.

9. When I *(be)* _____ in New York next week, I *(stay)* _____ at the Park Plaza Hotel.

10. Cindy and I *(go)* _____ to the beach tomorrow if the weather *(be)* _____ warm and sunny.

11. Jack *(watch)* _____ a football game on TV right now. As soon as the game *(be)* _____ over, he *(mow)* _____ the grass in the back yard.

12. As soon as the test *(be)* _____ over in class yesterday, the students *(leave)* _____ the room.

13. As soon as I *(get)* _____ home every day, my children always *(run)* _____ to the door to meet me.

14. A: I'll lend you my bike if I *(need, not)* _____ it tomorrow.
    B: Thanks.

15. A: Everyone in the office *(plan)* _____ to come to the annual company

     picnic tomorrow. *(you, come)* _____ ?

   B: Of course!

16. A: How *(you, get, usually)* _____ to work?

   B: I *(take)* _____ the commuter train every morning.

17. This morning, Bob *(comb)* _____ his hair when the comb *(break)*

   _____ . So he *(finish)* _____ combing his hair with his

   fingers and *(rush)* _____ out the door to class.

18. I'm exhausted! When I *(get)* _____ home tonight, I *(read)* _____

   _____ the paper and *(watch)* _____ the news. I *(do, not)*

   _____ any work around the house.

19. Yesterday I *(see)* _____ the man who stole the radio from my car last Friday. I

   (run) _____ after him, *(catch)* _____ him, and *(knock)*

   _____ him down. A passerby *(go)* _____ to call the police. I

   (sit) _____ on the man while I *(wait)* _____ for them to come.

   After they *(get)* _____ there and *(understand)* _____ the

   situation, they *(put)* _____ handcuffs on him and *(take)* _____

   him to jail.

20. A: My cousin *(have)* _____ a new cat. She now *(have)* _____

     four cats.

   B: Why *(she, have)* _____ so many?

   A: To catch the mice in her house.

   B: *(you, have)* _____ any cats?

   A: No, and I *(get, not)* _____ any. I *(have, not)* _____

     _____ mice in my house.

CHAPTER 4

The Present Perfect and the Past Perfect

◇ PRACTICE 1. Forms of the present perfect. (Charts 4-1 → 4-3)

Directions: Complete the dialogues with the given verbs and any words in parentheses. Use the present perfect.

1. *eat*　　A: (you, ever) ___Have you ever eaten___ pepperoni pizza?

　　　　　B: Yes, I ___have___ . I ___have eaten___ pepperoni pizza many times. OR

　　　　　No, I ___haven't___ . I (never) ___have never eaten___ pepperoni pizza.

2. *talk*　　A: (you, ever) _____ to a famous person?

　　　　　B: Yes, I _____ . I _____ to a lot of famous people. OR

　　　　　No, I _____ . I (never) _____ to a famous person.

3. *rent*　　A: (Erica, ever) _____ a car?

　　　　　B: Yes, she _____ . She _____ a car many times. OR

　　　　　No, she _____ . She (never) _____ a car.

4. *see*　　A: (you, ever) _____ a shooting star?

　　　　　B: Yes, I _____ . I _____ a lot of shooting stars. OR

　　　　　No, I _____ . I (never) _____ a shooting star.

5. *catch*　　A: (Joe, ever) _____ a big fish?

　　　　　B: Yes, he _____ . He _____ lots of big fish. OR

　　　　　No, he _____ . He (never) _____ a big fish.

6. *have* A: *(you, ever)* _____ a bad sunburn?

   B: Yes, I _____ . I _____ a bad sunburn several times. OR

   No, I _____ . I *(never)* _____ a bad

   sunburn.

◇ **PRACTICE 2. The present perfect. (Charts 4-1 → 4-3)**
   Directions: Complete the sentences with the present perfect of the verbs in parentheses.

   1. A cell phone is so convenient. I *(want)* _____**have wanted**_____ one since they were

      available for sale.

   2. I quit eating meat when I was in college. I *(be)* _____ a strict

      vegetarian for several years and feel very healthy.

   3. We got a dog because we live in an isolated area. She *(be)* _____ a

      wonderful watchdog for us.

   4. We *(fly)* _____ that airline many times because the service is excellent.

   5. Our neighbors *(pick up, not)* _____ their mail yet. They may

      not be back from their trip.

   6. Vivian *(change)* _____ her hair color so many times that no one can

      remember her natural color.

   7. Our teacher *(correct, already)* _____ our tests, but she

      (return, not) _____ them yet.

   8. A: Jose left two messages on my answering machine. I wonder what he wants.

      B: Maybe he just wants to talk. He said he *(talk, not)* _____

         to you in a long time.

   9. My parents *(need)* _____ a new car for several months. They *(look)*

      _____ in lots of car showrooms, but they can't agree on what kind of car

      to buy.

   10. A: *(you, have)* _____ your flu shot this year? I got mine last week.

       B: No, but I will. I *(get)* _____ one every year for the past three years.

          My doctor says it's a good idea after the age of 50.

◇ PRACTICE 3. Review: irregular verbs. (Charts 2-6, 2-7, and 4-1)
Directions: Write each verb in the correct group.

✓ring	put	quit	have	shut	teach
✓hurt	drink	stick	swim	sink	pay
✓win	stand	upset	find	let	bring
feed	keep	meet	sing	catch	set
weep	sit	cut	buy	fight	think

GROUP I. Simple form, simple past, and past participle are the same.

Example: cost → cost → cost

hurt	hurt	hurt

GROUP II. The vowel changes: i → a → u.

Example: begin → began → begun

ring	rang	rung

GROUP III. Simple past and past participle are the same.

Example: find → found → found

win	won	won

◇ **PRACTICE 4. The present perfect. (Charts 4-1 → 4-3)**
   Directions: Complete the sentences with the present perfect of the verbs in the list and any words in parentheses. Use each verb only once.

eat	look	save	✓use
give	play	sleep	wear
improve	rise	speak	win

1. People ____have used____ leather to make shoes for hundreds of years.

2. The night is over. It's daytime now. The sun _____ .

3. I *(never)* _____ golf, but I'd like to. It looks like fun.

4. Our team is great. They _____ all of their games so far this year. They haven't lost a single game.

5. Amy must be mad at me. She *(not)* _____ one word to me all evening. I wonder what I did to make her angry.

6. The cat must be sick. He *(not)* _____ any food for two days. We'd better call the vet.

7. Our teacher _____ us a lot of tests and quizzes since the beginning of the term.

8. We put a little money in our savings account every month. We want to buy a car, but we *(not)* _____ enough money yet. We'll have enough in a few more months.

9. *(you, ever)* _____ outdoors for an entire night? I mean without a tent, with nothing between you and the stars?

10. My aunt puts on a wig whenever she goes out, but I *(never)* _____ a wig in my whole life.

11. Paul's health _____ a lot since he started eating the right kinds of food, exercising regularly, and handling the stress in his life. He's never felt better.

12. I can't find my keys. I _____ everywhere—in all my pockets, in my briefcase, in my desk. They're gone.

◇ PRACTICE 5. The present perfect vs. the simple past. (Charts 4-3 and 4-4)
   Directions: Write F if the activity or situation is finished and C if it continues to the present.

1. __C__ My grandfather *has worked* since he was in high school.

2. __F__ My grandmother *worked* for 20 years.

3. __F__ I *finished* my work two hours ago.

4. __F__ I *have already finished* my work, so I'm leaving the office.

5. _____ My father *has been* sick since yesterday.

6. _____ Jane *was* sick last Monday.

7. _____ Tom *has already left.* He's not here.

8. _____ Tom *left* five minutes ago.

9. _____ I *have known* Max Shell since we were children.

10. _____ The baby *has had* a fever since midnight. I think I'll call the doctor.

11. _____ The baby *had* a fever all night, but he's better now.

12. _____ I *have had* the flu several times in my lifetime.

13. _____ I *had* the flu last year.

14. _____ Sue *has had* the flu since last Friday.

◇ PRACTICE 6. Review: irregular verbs. (Charts 2-6, 2-7, and 4-1)
   Directions: Complete the sentences with the simple past and the present perfect of the given verbs.

1. *begin*   I _____began_____ a new diet and exercise program last week. I

   _____have begun_____ lots of new diet and exercise programs in my lifetime.

2. *bend*   I _____ down to pick up my young son from his crib this morning. I

   _____ down to pick him up many times since he was born.

3. *broadcast*   The radio _____ news about a terrible earthquake in Iran

   last week. The radio _____ news about Iran every day

   since the earthquake occurred there.

4. *catch*   I _____ a cold last week. I _____ a lot

   of colds in my lifetime.

5. *come*   A tourist _____ into Mr. Nasser's jewelry store after lunch. A lot of

   tourists _____ into his store since he opened it last year.

6. *cut*   I _____ some flowers from my garden yesterday. I

   _____ lots of flowers from my garden so far this summer.

7. *dig*   The workers _____ a hole to fix the leak in the water pipe. They

   _____ many holes to fix water leaks since the earthquake.

8. *draw*   The artist _____ a picture of a sunset yesterday. She

_____ many pictures of sunsets in her lifetime.

9. *feed*   I _____ birds at the park yesterday. I _____ birds

at the park every day since I lost my job.

10. *fight*   We _____ a war last year. We _____ several

wars since we became an independent country.

11. *forget*   I _____ to turn off the stove after dinner. I _____

_____ to turn off the stove a lot of times in my lifetime.

12. *hide*   The children _____ in the basement yesterday. They _____

_____ in the basement often since they discovered a secret place there.

13. *hit*   The baseball player _____ the ball out of the stadium yesterday. He

_____ a lot of home runs since he joined our team.

14. *hold*   My husband _____ the door open for me when he entered the

restaurant. He _____ a door open for me many times since

we met each other.

15. *keep*   During the discussion yesterday, I _____ my opinion to myself. I

_____ my opinions to myself a lot of times in my lifetime.

16. *lead*   Mary _____ the group discussion at the conference. She

_____ group discussions many times since she started going to

conferences.

17. *lose*   Eddie _____ money at the racetrack yesterday. He _____

_____ money at the racetrack lots of times in his lifetime.

18. *meet*   I _____ two new people in my class yesterday. I _____
a lot of new people since I started going to school here.

19. *ride*   I _____ the bus to work yesterday. I _____
the bus to work many times since I got a job downtown.

20. *ring*   The doorbell _____ a few minutes ago. The doorbell _____
_____ three times so far today.

21. *see*   I _____ a good movie yesterday. I _____ a lot of
good movies in my lifetime.

22. *steal*   The fox _____ a chicken from the farmer's yard. The fox _____
_____ three chickens so far this month.

23. *stick*   I _____ a stamp on the corner of the envelope. I _____
_____ lots of stamps on envelopes in my lifetime.

24. *sweep*   I _____ the floor of my apartment yesterday. I _____
the floor of my apartment lots of times since I moved in.

25. *take*   I _____ a test yesterday. I _____ lots of tests in
my life as a student.

26. *upset*   The Smith children _____ Mr. Jordan when they broke his window.
Because they are careless and noisy, they _____ Mr. Jordan
many times since they moved in next door.

27. *withdraw*   I _____ some money from my bank account yesterday. I
_____ more than three hundred dollars from my
bank account so far this month.

28. *write*   I _____ a letter to a friend last night. I _____
lots of letters to my friends in my lifetime.

◇ PRACTICE 7. The present perfect vs. the simple past. (Chart 4-4)
Directions: Fill in the blanks with the present perfect or simple past form of the verb.

1. I *(go)* _____went_____ to Toronto last year for business. I *(go)* ___have gone___
there several times since then.

2. I *(live)* _____ in British Columbia from 1998 to 2000.

3. My friend, Joe, *(live)* _____ in Vancouver since 2000.

4. Before Joe *(move)* _____ to Vancouver, he *(work)* _____ on cruise ships as a cook.

5. My college roommate came from Ghana. We *(room)* _____ together for three years, and then she *(return)* _____ home.

6. My grandfather *(be)* _____ a great golfer for most of his life, but he *(die)* _____ last year.

7. My father *(play)* _____ competitive golf for most of his life and really enjoys it.

8. Since my husband began working the night shift, he *(sleep, not)* _____ very well.

9. When I lived in Alaska, the long daylight hours *(make)* _____ it difficult for me to sleep.

10. Since I was a child, I *(enjoy)* _____ collecting rocks from the beach.

11. When I was a child, my friends *(collect)* _____ rocks with me.

◇ **PRACTICE 8. Review: irregular verbs. (Charts 2-6, 2-7, and 4-1)**
Directions: This is a review of irregular verbs. Complete the sentences with the simple past or the present perfect of the given verbs and any words in parentheses.

1. *go*   a. I _____**have gone**_____ to every play at the local theater so far this year.

   b. My whole family _____**went**_____ to the play last weekend.

2. *give*   a. Jane _____**gave**_____ me a ride home from work today.

   b. *(she, ever)* _____**Has she ever given**_____ you a ride home since she started working in your department?

3. *fall*   a. I _____ down many times in my lifetime, but never hard enough to really hurt myself or break a bone.

   b. Mike _____ down many times during football practice yesterday.

4. *break*   a. *(you, ever)* _____ a bone in your body?

   b. I _____ my leg when I was ten years old. I jumped off the roof of my house.

5. *shake*   a. In my entire lifetime, I *(never)* _____ hands with a famous movie star.

   b. In 2000, I _____ hands with a famous soccer player.

6. *hear* a. I _____ you practicing your trumpet late last night.

b. In fact, I _____ you practicing every night for two weeks.

7. *fly* a. Mike is a commercial airline pilot. Yesterday he _____ from Tokyo to Los Angeles.

b. Mike _____ to many places in the world since he became a pilot.

8. *wear* a. Carol really likes her new leather jacket. She _____ it every day since she bought it.

b. She _____ her new leather jacket to the opera last night.

9. *build* a. *(you, ever)* _____ a piece of furniture?

b. My daughter _____ a table in her woodworking class at the high school last year.

10. *teach* a. Ms. Kent _____ math at the local high school since 1995.

b. She _____ in Hungary last year on an exchange program.

11. *find* a. In your lifetime, *(you, ever)* _____ something really valuable?

b. My sister _____ a very expensive diamond ring in the park last year.

12. *drive* a. After I took Danny to school, I _____ straight to work.

b. I'm an experienced driver, but I *(never)* _____ a bus or a big truck.

13. *sing*   a. I _____ a duet with my mother at the art benefit last night.

            b. We _____ together ever since I was a small child.

14. *run*   a. I *(never)* _____ in a marathon race, and I don't intend to.

            b. I'm out of breath because I _____ all the way over here.

15. *tell*   a. Last night, my brother _____ me a secret.

            b. He _____ me lots of secrets in his lifetime.

16. *stand*   a. When I visited the United Nations last summer, I _____ in the

               main gallery and felt a great sense of history.

            b. Many great world leaders _____ there over the years.

17. *spend*   a. I _____ all of my money at the mall yesterday.

            b. I don't have my rent money this month. I *(already)* _____

               _____ it on other things.

18. *make*   a. I consider myself fortunate because I _____ many good

               friends in my lifetime.

            b. I _____ a terrible mistake last night. I forgot that my friend had

               invited me to his apartment for dinner.

19. *rise*   a. The price of flour _____ a lot since February.

            b. When his name was announced, Jack _____ from his seat and

               walked to the podium to receive his award.

20. *feel*   a. I _____ terrible yesterday, so I stayed in bed.

            b. I _____ terrible for a week now. I'd better see a doctor.

◇ **PRACTICE 9. SINCE vs. FOR. (Chart 4-5)**
   Directions: Complete the sentences with *since* or *for*.

1. David has worked for the power company ____since____ 1999.

2. His brother has worked for the power company ____for____ five years.

3. I have known Peter Gow _____ September.

4. I've known his sister _____ three months.

5. Jonas has walked with a limp _____ many years.

6. He's had a bad leg _____ he was in the war.

7. Rachel hasn't been in class _____ last Tuesday.

8. She hasn't been in class _____ three days.

9. My vision has improved _____ I got new reading glasses.

10. I've had a toothache _____ yesterday morning.

11. I've had this toothache _____ thirty-six hours.

12. I've had a cold _____ almost a week.

13. Jane hasn't worked _____ last summer when the factory closed down.

14. I attended Jefferson Elementary School _____ six years.

◇ **PRACTICE 10. Present perfect with SINCE and FOR. (Chart 4-5)**
Directions: Rewrite the sentences using *since* or *for*.

1. I was in this class a month ago, and I am in this class now.
   → *I have been in this class for a month.*

2. I knew my teacher in September, and I know her now.

3. Sam wanted a dog two years ago, and he wants one now.

4. Sara needed a new car last year, and she still needs one.

5. Our professor was sick a week ago, and she is still sick.

6. They live in Canada. They moved there in December.

7. I know Mrs. Brown. I met her in 1999.

8. Tom works at a fast-food restaurant. He got the job three weeks ago.

◇ **PRACTICE 11. Present perfect and simple past with time words. (Charts 4-1 → 4-5)**
Directions: Check all the phrases that correctly complete the sentences. Mark those that don't with a dash. The first item has been started for you.

1. The Petersons took a trip

   ___✓___ two weeks ago.

   ___−___ since yesterday.

   ___✓___ yesterday.

   _____ last year.

   _____ several months ago.

   _____ since last month.

   _____ the day before yesterday.

   _____ in March.

2. The Petersons have been out of town

   _____ the day before yesterday.

   _____ one month ago.

   _____ since Friday.

   _____ last week.

   _____ since last week.

   _____ in April last year.

   _____ several weeks ago.

   _____ for several weeks.

◇ PRACTICE 12. SINCE-clauses. (Chart 4-5)
   Directions: Complete the sentences with the words in parentheses. Use the present perfect or the simple past.

   1. Carol and I are old friends. I *(know)* __have known__ her since I *(be)* ____was____ a freshman in high school.

   2. Maria *(have)* _____ a lot of problems since she *(come)* _____ to this country.

   3. I *(experience, not)* _____ any problems since I *(come)* _____ here.

   4. Since the semester *(begin)* _____, our teacher *(give)* _____ four tests.

   5. Mike *(be)* _____ in school since he *(be)* _____ six years old.

   6. My mother *(be, not)* _____ in school since she *(graduate)* _____ from college in 1978.

   7. Since I *(start)* _____ doing this exercise, I *(complete)* _____ six sentences.

   8. Since soccer season *(begin)* _____, our son *(have, not)* _____ _____ much free time.

   9. Our long-distance phone calls *(become)* _____ less expensive since we *(change)* _____ to a different telephone company.

   10. Our phone bill *(rise)* _____ since we *(buy)* _____ a cell phone.

◇ PRACTICE 13. The present perfect progressive. (Charts 4-6 and 4-7)
   Directions: Use the given information to complete the dialogues. Use the present perfect progressive.

   1. Eric is studying. He started to **study** at seven o'clock. It is now nine o'clock.
      A: How long __has Eric been studying_____?
      B: He _'s been studying_____ for __two hours_____.

   2. Kathy is working at the computer. She began to **work** at the computer at two o'clock. It is now three o'clock.
      A: How long __has Kathy been working at the computer_____?
      B: She _'s been working_____ since __two o'clock_____.

3. It began to **rain** two days ago. It is still raining.

    A: How long _____ ?

    B: It _____ for _____ .

4. Liz is reading. She began to **read** at ten o'clock. It is now ten-thirty.

    A: How long _____ ?

    B: She _____ for _____ .

5. Boris began to **study** English in 2001. He is still studying English.

    A: How long _____ ?

    B: He _____ since _____ .

6. Three months ago, Nicole started to **work** at the Silk Road Clothing Store.

    A: How long _____ ?

    B: She _____ for _____ .

7. Ms. Rice started to **teach** at this school in September 2001.

    A: How long _____ ?

    B: She _____ since _____ .

8. Mr. Fisher **drives** a Chevy. He bought it twelve years ago.

    A: How long _____ ?

    B: He _____ for _____ .

9. Mrs. Taylor is **waiting** to see her doctor. She arrived at the waiting room at two o'clock. It is now three-thirty.

    A: How long _____ ?

    B: She _____ for _____ .

10. Ted and Erica started to **play** tennis at two o'clock. It's now four-thirty.

    A: How long _____ ?

    B: They _____ since _____ .

◇ PRACTICE 14. The present perfect progressive. (Charts 4-6 and 4-7)
Directions: Choose the correct verb form.

1. Where have you been? I _____ for you for over an hour!
    A. am waiting   (B.) have been waiting

2. I'm exhausted! I _____ for the last eight hours without a break.
    A. am working   B. have been working

3. Shhh! Susan _____ . Let's not make any noise. We don't want to wake her up.
    A. is sleeping   B. has been sleeping

4. Annie, go upstairs and wake your brother up. He _____ for over ten hours. He has chores to do.
   A. is sleeping   B. has been sleeping

5. Erin has never gone camping. She _____ in a tent.
   A. has never slept   B. has never been sleeping

6. This is a great shirt! I _____ it at least a dozen times, and it still looks like new.
   A. have washed   B. have been washing

7. Aren't you about finished with the dishes? You _____ dishes for thirty minutes or more. How long can it take to wash dishes?
   A. have washed   B. have been washing

8. We _____ to the Steak House restaurant many times. The food is excellent.
   A. have gone   B. have been going

◇ **PRACTICE 15. ALREADY, STILL, YET, ANYMORE.** (Chart 4-8)
   Directions: Choose the correct completion.

1. I haven't finished my homework yet. I'm _____ working on it.
   A. already   B. still   C. yet   D. anymore

2. *Top Rock Videos* used to be my favorite TV show, but I have stopped watching it. I don't watch it _____ .
   A. already   B. still   C. yet   D. anymore

3. I don't have to take any more math classes. I've _____ taken all the required courses.
   A. already   B. still   C. yet   D. anymore

4. I used to nearly choke in an airplane because of all the smoke in the cabin. But smoking is now forbidden by law on all domestic flights. You can't smoke in an airplane _____ .
   A. already   B. still   C. yet   D. anymore

5. I'm not quite ready to leave. I haven't finished packing my suitcase _____ .
   A. already   B. still   C. yet   D. anymore

6. "Don't you have a class at two?"
   "Yeah, why?"
   "Look at your watch."
   "Oh my gosh, it's _____ past two! Bye!"
   A. already   B. still   C. yet   D. anymore

7. Don't sit there! I painted that chair yesterday, and the paint isn't completely dry _____ .
   A. already   B. still   C. yet   D. anymore

8. 1448 South 45th Street is Joe's old address. He doesn't live there _____ .
   A. already   B. still   C. yet   D. anymore

9. Mr. Wood is eighty-eight years old, but he _____ goes into his office every day.
   A. already   B. still   C. yet   D. anymore

10. "Are you going to drive to Woodville with us for the street festival Saturday?"
    "I don't know. I might. I haven't made up my mind _____."
       A. already   B. still   C. yet   D. anymore

◇ **PRACTICE 16. ALREADY, STILL, YET, ANYMORE.   (Chart 4-8)**
   Directions: Complete the sentences with *already*, *yet*, *still*, or *anymore*.

   1. A: Has Dennis graduated _____yet_____ ?

      B: No. He's still in school.

   2. A: I'm hungry. How about you? Did you eat _____ ?

      B: No. Did you?

      A: Nope. Let's go eat lunch.

   3. A: Do you _____ live on Fifth Street?

      B: Not anymore. I moved.

   4. A: Has Karen found a new apartment _____ ?

      B: Not that I know of. She's still living on Elm Street.

   5. A: Do you _____ love me?

      B: Of course I do! I love you very much.

   6. A: Is the baby _____ sleeping?

      B: Yes. Shhh. We don't want to wake him up.

   7. A: Is the baby asleep _____ ?

      B: I think so. I don't hear anything from the nursery. I put him down for his nap fifteen

         minutes ago, so I'm pretty sure he's asleep by now.

   8. It started raining an hour ago. We can't go for a walk because it's _____

      raining. I hope it stops soon.

   9. Look! The rain has stopped. It isn't raining _____ . Let's go for a walk.

   10. I didn't understand this chapter in my biology book when I read it yesterday. Since then, I've

       read it three more times, but I _____ don't understand it.

   11. A: Is Anne home _____ ?

       B: No, she isn't. I'm getting worried. She was supposed to be home at eight. It's almost

          nine, and she _____ isn't here.

       A: Don't worry. She'll probably be here any minute.

12. A: I'm going to have another sandwich.

    B: What? You just ate three sandwiches!

    A: I know, but I'm not full _____ . I'm _____ hungry.

13. A: Would you like to see today's newspaper?

    B: Thanks, but I've _____ read it.

14. A: Did you try to call Peter again?

    B: Yes, but the line was _____ busy. I'll try again in a few minutes.

15. A: How does Dick like his job at the cafe?

    B: He doesn't work there _____ . He found a new job.

16. A: Is your younger sister a college student?

    B: No. She's _____ in high school.

17. A: When are you going to make Tommy's birthday cake?

    B: I've _____ made it.

18. A: How did you do on your calculus exam?

    B: I haven't taken it _____ . The exam is tomorrow. I'm _____

    studying for it.

◇ PRACTICE 17. Verb tense review. (Chapters 1 → 4)
Directions: Read the conversation between Ann and Ben. Complete the sentences with the words in parentheses.

BEN: I *(need)* _____need_____ to find a job. Where *(be)* _____ a good place for a
                        1   2

   student to work?

ANN: *(you, work, ever)* _____ at a restaurant?
                                              3

BEN: Yes. I *(work)* _____
                        4

   at several restaurants. I *(have)*

   _____ a job as a
             5

   dishwasher last fall.

ANN: Where?

BEN: At The Bistro, a little cafe on First Street.

ANN: How long *(you, work)* _____ there?
                                             6

BEN: For two months.

ANN: I *(work)* _____ in a lot of restaurants, but I *(have, never)*
                        7

_____ a dishwashing job. How *(you, like)*
          8

_____ your job as a dishwasher?
          9

BEN: I *(like, not)* _____ it very much. It *(be)* _____ hard
                              10   11

work for low pay.

ANN: Where *(you, work)* _____ at present?
                                    12

BEN: I *(have, not)* _____ a job right now. I *(have, not)*
                            13

_____ a job since I *(quit)* _____ the dishwashing one.
          14   15

ANN: *(you, look)* _____ for a part-time or a full-time job?
                          16

BEN: A part-time job, maybe twenty hours a week.

ANN: I *(go)* _____ to Al's Place tomorrow to see about a job. The restaurant
                    17

(look) _____ for help. Why don't you come along with me?
                18

BEN: Thanks. I think I *(do)* _____ that. I *(look, never)*
                                      19

_____ for a job at Al's Place before. Maybe the pay *(be)*
          20

_____ better than at The Bistro.
        21

ANN: I *(know, not)* _____ . We *(find)* _____ out when
                            22   23

we *(go)* _____ there tomorrow.
                24

◇ **PRACTICE 18. The present perfect vs. the past perfect. (Chart 4-9)**
Directions: Complete the sentences with the word in parentheses. Use the present perfect or the
past perfect.

1. I am not hungry. I *(eat, already)* ____*have already eaten*____ .

2. I was not hungry. I *(eat, already)* ____*had already eaten*____ .

3. It's ten o'clock. I *(finish, already)* _____ my

homework, so I'm going to go to bed.

4. Last night I went to bed at ten o'clock. I *(finish, already)* _____
   my homework.

5. By the time* I went to bed last night, I *(finish, already)* _____
   my homework.

6. Sam's parties usually start late, so I was surprised that his party *(start, already)* _____
   _____ by the time I got there.

7. Look at all the people who are here! The party *(start, already)* _____
   _____ .

8. Carol missed her plane yesterday because of a traffic jam on her way to the airport. By the
   time she got to the airport, her plane *(leave, already)* _____ .

◇ PRACTICE 19. The past progressive vs. the past perfect. (Chart 4-9)
   Directions: Complete the sentences with the words in parentheses. Use the past progressive or the
   past perfect.

   1. When I left for school this morning, it *(rain)* ____was raining____ , so I used my
      umbrella.

   2. By the time class was over this morning, the rain *(stop)* ____had stopped____ , so I
      didn't need my umbrella anymore.

   3. Last night I started to study at 7:30. Dick came at 7:35. I *(study)* _____
      when Dick came.

   4. Last night I started to study at 7:30. I finished studying at 9:00. Dan came at 9:30. By the
      time Dan came, I *(finish)* _____ my homework.

   5. When I walked into the kitchen after dinner last night, my wife *(wash)* _____
      the dishes, so I picked up a dish towel to help her.

   6. By the time I walked into the kitchen after dinner tonight, my husband *(wash, already)*
      _____ the dishes and *(put)* _____ them
      away.

   _____

   *by the time = before.

◇ PRACTICE 20. The past perfect. (Chart 4-9)

Directions: Read the passage and <u>underline</u> the past perfect verbs and their modifying adverbs **always** and **never**. Then complete the sentences that follow the passage. Use the past perfect in your completions.

(1) Alan Green got married for the first time at age 49. His new life is very different because he has had to change many old habits. For example, before his marriage, he <u>had always watched</u> TV during dinner, but his wife likes to talk at dinnertime, so now the TV is off.

(2) Until his marriage, Alan had always read the front page of the newspaper first, but his wife likes to read the front page first, too, so now Alan reads the sports page first.

(3) Until he got married, he had never let anyone else choose the radio station in the car. He had always listened to exactly what he wanted to listen to. But his wife likes to choose what's on the radio when she's in the car with him.

(4) When he was a bachelor, Alan had always left his dirty socks on the floor. Now he picks them up and puts them in the laundry basket.

(5) Before he was married, he'd never put the cap back on the toothpaste. He left it off. His wife prefers to have the cap back on. She also squeezes from the bottom of the tube, and Alan doesn't. Alan can't remember to put the cap back on, so now they have separate toothpaste tubes.

(6) Alan had never shared the TV remote control with anyone before he got married. He still likes to have control of the TV remote, but he doesn't say anything when his wife uses it.

Complete these sentences.

1. Until Alan got married, he _____*had always watched*_____ TV during dinner.

2. Before his marriage, he _____ the front page of the newspaper first.

3. Prior to getting married, he _____ other people choose the station on his car radio.

4. Until he began married life, he _____ his dirty socks on the floor.

5. Before getting married, he _____ the toothpaste cap back on.

6. Until he had a wife who also liked to use the TV remote control, he _____ _____ the remote with anyone.

◇ PRACTICE 21. Verb tense review. (Chapters 2 and 4)

Directions: Complete the sentences with the words in parentheses.

1. A: *(you, enjoy)* ___Did you enjoy___ the concert last night?

   B: Very much. I *(go, not)* ___hadn't gone___ to a concert in a long time.

2. A: *(you, see)* _____ John yesterday?

   B: Yes, I did. It *(be)* _____ good to see him again. I *(see, not)*

   _____ him in a long time.

3. A: Hi, Jim! It's good to see you again. I *(see, not)* _____ you in weeks.

   B: Hi, Sue! It *(be)* _____ good to see you again, too. I *(see, not)*

   _____ you since the end of last semester. How's everything going?

4. A: *(you, get)* _____ to class on time yesterday morning?

   B: No. By the time I *(get)* _____ there, it *(begin, already)* _____

   _____ .

5. A: I called Ana, but I couldn't talk to her.

   B: Why not?

   A: She *(go, already)* _____ to bed, and her sister didn't

   want to wake her up for a phone call.

6. A: You're a wonderful artist. I love your watercolor paintings of the river valley.

   B: Thank you. I *(paint)* _____ the same valley many times because

   it has such interesting light at different times of the day.

7. A: I had a scare yesterday. I *(watch)* _____ the news when a

   tornado warning flashed on the screen.

   B: What *(you, do)* _____ ?

   A: I *(run)* _____ to the basement of the house.

8. A: *(you, go)* _____ out to eat last night?

   B: No. By the time I *(get)* _____ home, my husband *(make, already)*

   _____ dinner for us.

   A: How *(be)* _____ it?

   B: Terrific! We *(have)* _____ chicken, rice, and a salad. While we *(eat)*

   _____ , George Drake *(stop)* _____ by to visit us,

   so we *(invite)* _____ him to join us for dinner.

◇ PRACTICE 22. Error analysis. (Chapters 1 → 4)
Directions: Correct the errors.

1. Where have you been? I've ^{been} waiting for you for an hour.

2. Anna have been a soccer fan since a long time.

3. Since I have been a child, I liked to solve puzzles.

4. Have you ever want to travel around the world?

5. The family is at the hospital since they hear about the accident.

6. My sister is only 30 years old, but her hair has began to turn gray.

7. Jake has been working as a volunteer at the children's hospital several times.

8. Steve has worn his black suit only once since he has bought it.

9. My cousin is studying for medical school exams since last month.

10. The students are hearing rumors about their teacher's engagement for a week.

11. I don't know the results of my medical tests already. I'll find out soon.

12. Jean has been try to get online to go Internet shopping for an hour.

13. By the time Michelle unlocked the door and got into her apartment, the phone already

    stopped ringing.

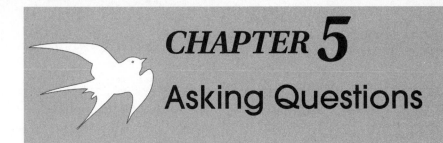

CHAPTER 5
Asking Questions

◇ **PRACTICE 1. Preview: asking questions.** (Charts 5-1 → 5-13)

Directions: Pretend that you are interviewing Anna, a member of your class. Write your name on the first line, and then complete the dialogue with appropriate questions.

1.   ME: Hi. My name is _____ . Our teacher has asked me to interview you so that I can practice asking questions. Could I ask you a few questions about yourself?

   ANNA: Sure.

2.   ME: Well, first of all, ___what is your name_____ ?

   ANNA: Anna.

3.   ME: _____ ?

   ANNA: Yes, that's my first name.

4.   ME: _____ ?

   ANNA: Polanski.

5.   ME: _____ ?

   ANNA: P-O-L-A-N-S-K-I.

   ME: Let me make sure I have that right. Your first name is Anna, A-N-N-A. And your last name is Polanski, P-O-L-A-N-S-K-I. Right?

   ANNA: That's right.

6.   ME: _____ ?

   ANNA: Poland.

7.   ME: _____ ?

   ANNA: Warsaw. My hometown is Warsaw.

8.   ME: _____ ?

   ANNA: Two weeks ago. I came to this country two weeks ago.

9.   ME: _____ ?

   ANNA: To study. I came here because I wanted to study at this school.

10. ME: _____ ?

   ANNA: Biochemistry.

11. ME: _____ ?

    ANNA: I'm going to stay here for four years, or until I graduate.

12. ME: _____ ?

    ANNA: I'm living at my aunt and uncle's house.

13. ME: _____ ?

    ANNA: No, it isn't far from school.

14. ME: _____ ?

    ANNA: I'd say about ten blocks.

15. ME: _____ ?

    ANNA: Sometimes I take the bus, but usually I walk.

16. ME: You're lucky. I live far away from the school, so it takes me a long time to get here
    every day. But that's my only big complaint about living here. Otherwise, I like
    going to this school a lot. _____ ?

    ANNA: Very much.

    ME: Well, thanks for the interview. I think I have enough information for the assignment.
    Nice to meet you.

    ANNA: Nice to meet you, too.

◇ PRACTICE 2. Yes/no questions. (Chart 5-1)*

Directions: Write the correct question form. Use the information in B's response to create each
question.

		helping verb	subject	main verb	rest of sentence
1. SIMPLE PRESENT	A:	Do	you	like	coffee?
	B: Yes, I like coffee.				

		helping verb	subject	main verb	rest of sentence
2. SIMPLE PRESENT	A:	_____	_____	_____	_____
	B: Yes, Tom likes coffee.				

		helping verb	subject	main verb	rest of sentence
3. PRESENT PROGRESSIVE	A:	_____	_____	_____	_____
	B: Yes, Ann is watching TV.				

		helping verb	subject	main verb	rest of sentence
4. PRESENT PROGRESSIVE	A:	_____	_____	_____	_____
	B: Yes, I'm having lunch with Rob.				

Question forms of tenses and modals can be found in the following charts in the *FEG 3e* student book:
    Simple present and present progressive: Chart 1-2, p. 4
    Simple past: Chart 2-2, p. 26
    Past progressive: Chart 2-9, p. 39
    Simple future: Charts 3-2, p. 56, and 3-3, p. 59
    Modal *can:* Chart 7-2, p. 191

	helping verb	subject	main verb	rest of sentence

5. SIMPLE   A: _____ _____ _____ _____
   PAST   B: Yes, Sara walked to school.

	helping verb	subject	main verb	rest of sentence

6. PAST   A: _____ _____ _____ _____
   PROGRESSIVE B: Yes, Ann was taking a nap.

	helping verb	subject	main verb	rest of sentence

7. SIMPLE   A: _____ _____ _____ _____
   FUTURE   B: Yes, Ted will come to the meeting.

	helping verb	subject	main verb	rest of sentence

8. MODAL: *CAN* A: _____ _____ _____ _____
                 B: Yes, Rita can ride a bicycle.

	form of *be*	subject	rest of sentence

9. MAIN VERB: *BE*   A: _____ _____ _____
   SIMPLE   B: Yes, Ann is a good artist.
   PRESENT

	form of *be*	subject	rest of sentence

10. MAIN VERB: *BE*   A: _____ _____ _____
    SIMPLE PAST   B: Yes, I was at the wedding.

◇ **PRACTICE 3. Yes/no questions and short answers.** (Charts 5-1 and 5-2)
   Directions: Complete Speaker A's questions with **do**, **does**, **is**, or **are**. Complete Speaker B's short answers.

1. A: I need a flashlight. _____Do_____ you have one?
   B: No, _____I don't_____ .

2. A: _____ Africa the largest continent?
   B: No, _____ . Asia is.

3. A: _____ ants eat other insects?
   B: Yes, _____ .

4. A: _____ you going to be in class tomorrow?
   B: Yes, _____ .

5. A: _____ all snakebites poisonous?
   B: No, _____ .

6. A: _____ crocodiles lay eggs?
   B: Yes, _____ .

7. A: _____ it raining right now?

   B: No, _____ .

8. A: _____ that pen belong to you?

   B: No, _____ .

9. A: _____ you working on English grammar right now?

   B: Yes, _____ .

10. A: Mercury is a liquid metal used in thermometers. _____ mercury have a boiling

    point?

    B: Yes, _____ . It boils at 356.58°C.

◇ **PRACTICE 4. Yes/no questions and short answers.** (Charts 5-1 and 5-2)
   Directions: Answer the questions honestly. Use short answers.

   1. Do you know how to swim? _____*Yes, I do.*___ OR ___*No, I don't.*_____

   2. Does your mother speak Chinese? _____

   3. Are you going downtown tomorrow? _____

   4. Will you be in class tomorrow? _____

   5. Can you play the guitar? _____

   6. Do you know how to play the violin? _____

   7. Are we going to have a test on grammar tomorrow? _____

   8. Can turtles swim? _____

   9. Should people smoke cigarettes? _____

   10. Did you watch TV last night? _____

   11. Do you have a bicycle? _____

   12. Will class begin on time tomorrow? _____

   13. Does class begin on time every day? _____

   14. Were all of the students in class yesterday? _____

   15. Should the teacher speak more slowly? _____

   16. Is English grammar easy? _____

   17. Was this exercise difficult? _____

◇ **PRACTICE 5. Yes/no questions and short answers. (Charts 5-1 and 5-2)**
   Directions: Complete Speaker A's questions. Complete Speaker B's short answers.

1. A: _____Does Jane eat_____ lunch at the cafeteria every day?
   B: Yes, _____she does._____ (Jane eats lunch at the cafeteria every day.)

2. A: _____Do_____ your parents live nearby?
   B: No, _____ (My parents don't live nearby.)

3. A: _____ to class yesterday?
   B: No, _____ (Ann and Jim didn't come to class yesterday.)

4. A: _____ in your grammar workbook?
   B: Yes, _____ (I'm writing in my grammar workbook.)

5. A: _____ home last night?
   B: No, _____ (I wasn't home last night.)

6. A: _____ in your astronomy class?
   B: Yes, _____ (Tim Wilson is in my astronomy class.)

7. A: _____ her work before she goes to bed?
   B: Yes, _____ (Karen will finish her work before she goes to bed.)

8. A: _____ under water?
   B: Yes, _____ (Some birds can swim under water.)

9. A: _____ at your homework for tomorrow yet?
   B: No, _____ (I haven't looked at my homework for tomorrow yet.)

◇ **PRACTICE 6. Yes/no and information questions. (Charts 5-1 and 5-2)**
   Directions: Complete the dialogues by writing Speaker A's questions. Write Ø if no word is needed in a space.

1.
(question word)	helping verb	subject	main verb	rest of sentence
A: Ø	Did	you	hear	the news yesterday?

   B: Yes, I did. (I heard the news yesterday.)

2.
(question word)	helping verb	subject	main verb	rest of sentence
A: When	did	you	hear	the news?

   B: Yesterday. (I heard the news yesterday.)

3.
(question word)	helping verb	subject	main verb	rest of sentence
A: Ø	_____	_____	_____	_____

   B: Yes, he is. (Eric is reading today's paper.)

4.
(question word)	helping verb	subject	main verb	rest of sentence
A: _____	_____	_____	_____	Ø

   B: Today's paper. (Eric is reading today's paper.)

5.

(question word)	helping verb	subject	main verb	rest of sentence
A: _____ _____ _____ _____ _____

B: Yes, I did. (I found my wallet.)

6.

(question word)	helping verb	subject	main verb	rest of sentence
A: _____ _____ _____ _____ _____

B: On the floor of the car. (I found my wallet on the floor of the car.)

7.

(question word)	helping verb	subject	main verb	rest of sentence
A: _____ _____ _____ _____ _____

B: Because he enjoys the exercise. (Mr. Li walks to work because he enjoys the exercise.)

8.

(question word)	helping verb	subject	main verb	rest of sentence
A: _____ _____ _____ _____ _____

B: Yes, he does. (Mr. Li walks to work.)

9.

(question word)	helping verb	subject	main verb	rest of sentence
A: _____ _____ _____ _____ _____

B: Yes, she will. (Ms. Cook will return to her office at one o'clock.)

10.

(question word)	helping verb	subject	main verb	rest of sentence
A: _____ _____ _____ _____ _____

B: At one o'clock. (Ms. Cook will return to her office at one o'clock.)

11.

(question word)	form of *be*	subject	rest of sentence
A: _____ _____ _____ _____

B: Yes, it is. (The orange juice is in the refrigerator.)

12.

(question word)	form of *be*	subject	rest of sentence
A: _____ _____ _____ _____

B: In the refrigerator. (The orange juice is in the refrigerator.)

◇ PRACTICE 7. Information questions. (Charts 5-1 → 5-3)

Directions: Create questions for the given answers. Use the information in parentheses. Use **when, what time, where,** or **why.** Pay special attention to the word order in the questions.

1. A: _____ What time (when) do the fireworks start _____ this evening?

    B: 9:30. (The fireworks start at 9:30 this evening.)

2. A: _____ to see the principal?

    B: Because I need to get his signature on this application form. (I'm waiting to see the principal because I need to get his signature on this application form.)

3. A: _____ her new job?

    B: Next Monday morning. (Rachel starts her new job next Monday morning.)

4. A: _____ home for work?

   B: Usually around 6:00. (I usually leave home for work around 6:00.)

5. A: _____ to the meeting?

   B: Because I fell asleep after dinner and didn't wake up until 9:00. (I didn't get to the meeting because I fell asleep after dinner and didn't wake up until 9:00.)

6. A: _____ razor blades?

   B: At many different kinds of stores. (You can find razor blades at many different kinds of stores.)

7. A: _____ for home?

   B: Next Saturday. (I'm leaving for home next Saturday.)

8. A: _____ to finish this project?

   B: Next month. (I expect to finish this project next month.)

9. A: _____ ?

   B: To Mars. (The spaceship will go to Mars.)

10. A: _____ Chinese?

    B: In Germany. (I studied Chinese in Germany.)

    A: _____ Chinese in Germany?

    B: Because there is a good Chinese language school there.
    (I studied Chinese in Germany because there is a good Chinese language school there.)

    A: _____ to China to study Chinese?

    B: Because I had a scholarship to study in Germany.
    (I didn't go to China to study Chinese because I had a scholarship to study in Germany.)

◇ PRACTICE 8. Information questions. (Charts 5-1 → 5-3)
   Directions: Create information questions. Use *where, why, when,* or *what time.*

   1. A: ____When/What time did you get up____ this morning?

      B: At 7:30. (I got up at 7:30 this morning.)

   2. A: _____ today?

      B: At the cafeteria. (I ate lunch at the cafeteria today.)

   3. A: _____ lunch?

      B: At 12:15. (I ate lunch at 12:15.)

   4. A: _____ at the cafeteria?

      B: Because the food is good. (I eat lunch at the cafeteria because the food is good.)

5. A: _____?

   B: In Chicago. (My aunt and uncle live in Chicago.)

6. A: _____ your aunt and uncle?

   B: Next week. (I'm going to visit my aunt and uncle next week.)

7. A: _____ tonight?

   B: Around six. (I'll get home around six tonight.)

8. A: _____ tonight?

   B: At the library. (George is going to study at the library tonight.)

9. A: _____ at the library?

   B: Because it's quiet. (George studies at the library because it's quiet.)

10. A: _____ a bus?

    B: At that corner. (You can catch a bus at that corner.)

11. A: _____?

    B: Ten o'clock. (I have to leave at ten o'clock.)

12. A: _____ in 1998?

    B: In Japan. (I was living in Japan in 1998.)

13. A: _____ in their books?

    B: Because they're working on an exercise. (The students are writing in their books because they're working on an exercise.)

14. A: _____ you?

    B: Around seven. (You should call me around seven.)

15. A: _____ absent?

    B: Because she's flying her kite in the park. (Yoko is absent because she's flying her kite in the park.)

◇ PRACTICE 9. Information questions with WHY. (Charts 5-1 → 5-3)
Directions: Practice questions with **why**.

1. A: I was absent from class yesterday.

   B: Why _____were you_____ absent from class yesterday?

2. A: I can't come to your party this weekend.

   B: Why _____ to my party this weekend?

3. A: Tom went downtown yesterday.

   B: Why _____ downtown yesterday?

4. A: Ann won't be in class tomorrow.

   B: Why _____ in class tomorrow?

5. A: I need to go to the drugstore.

   B: Why _____ to go to the drugstore?

6. A: I'm going to buy a new dictionary.

   B: Why _____ a new dictionary?

7. A: I didn't do my homework last night.

   B: Why _____ your homework last night?

8. A: Anita is not coming to class tomorrow.

   B: Why _____ to class tomorrow?

9. A: Joe and I are going to the bank after class.

   B: Why _____ to the bank after class?

10. A: I didn't eat breakfast this morning

    B: Why _____ breakfast this morning?

11. A: Jack took a taxi to school today.

    B: Why _____ a taxi to school today?

12. A: I don't like the weather in this city.

    B: Why _____ the weather in this city?

◇ **PRACTICE 10. WHO, WHO(M), and WHAT. (Chart 5-4)**
   Directions: Create questions with **who**, **who(m)**, and **what**.

	QUESTION	ANSWER
1.	*Who knows Tom?*	**Someone** knows Tom.
2.	*Who(m) does Tom know?*	Tom knows **someone**.
3.	_____	**Someone** will help us.
4.	_____	I will ask **someone**.
5.	_____	Eric is talking to **someone** on the phone.
6.	_____	**Someone** is knocking on the door.
7.	_____	**Something** surprised them.
8.	_____	Jack said **something**.
9.	_____	Sue talked about **something**.
10.	_____	Ann talked about **someone**.

◇ **PRACTICE 11. WHO, WHO(M), and WHAT. (Chart 5-4)**

Directions: Complete the dialogues by creating questions. Use the information in the long answer in parentheses to create each question.

1. A: ___Who taught_____ you to play chess?

    B: My mother. (My mother taught me to play chess.)

2. A: _____?

    B: A bank robbery. (Robert saw a bank robbery.)

3. A: _____ a good look at the bank robber?

    B: Robert did. (Robert got a good look at the bank robber.)

4. A: _____?

    B: A toy for my brother's children. (I'm making a toy for my brother's children.)

5. A: _____ to?

    B: Joe. (That calculator belongs to Joe.)

6. A: _____ in your pocket?

    B: A bag of candy. (I have a bag of candy in my pocket.)

7. A: _____?

    B: A mouse. (The cat killed a mouse.)

8. A: _____?

    B: Curiosity. (Curiosity killed the cat.*)

9. A: _____ an apple fall to the ground from a tree?

    B: Gravity. (Gravity makes an apple fall to the ground from a tree.)

10. A: _____ on the envelope?

    B: My sister. (My sister wrote a note on the envelope.)

11. A: _____ from?

    B: My father. (I got a letter from my father.)

_____

Curiosity is the desire to learn about something. "Curiosity killed the cat" is an English saying that means we can get into trouble when we want to know too much about something that doesn't really concern us.

◇ PRACTICE 12. Asking for the meaning of a word. (Charts 5-3 and 5-4)
   Directions: Ask for the meaning of the words in *italics*. Complete the dialogue.

   1. Captain Cook *explored* many islands in the Pacific Ocean.

      A: ___What does "explore" mean?_____

      B: It means ___"to go to a new place and find out about it."_____

   2. Alice put her hand *underneath* the blanket.

      A: _____

      B: It means _____

   3. How many times a minute do people *blink?*

      A: _____

      B: It means _____

   4. The food was absolutely *delicious!*

      A: _____

      B: It means _____

◇ PRACTICE 13. WHAT + a form of DO. (Chart 5-6)
   Directions: Use the information in parentheses to make questions with ***what*** + a form of ***do*** to complete each dialogue. Use the same verb tense or modal that is used in the parentheses.

   1. A: ___What is Alex doing_____ ?

      B: Watching a movie on TV. (Alex <u>is watching</u> a movie on TV.)

   2. A: ___What should I do_____ if someone calls while you're out?

      B: Just take a message. (You <u>should take</u> a message if someone calls while I'm out.)

   3. A: _____ ?

      B: They explore space. (Astronauts <u>explore</u> space.)

   4. A: _____ Saturday morning?

      B: Play tennis at Waterfall Park. (I'<u>m going to play</u> tennis at Waterfall Park Saturday morning.)

   5. A: _____ when you get sick?

      B: I see my doctor. (I <u>see</u> my doctor when I get sick.)

   6. A: _____ to help you?

      B: Carry this suitcase. (You <u>can carry</u> this suitcase to help me.)

   7. A: _____ when she heard the good news?

      B: She smiled. (Sara <u>smiled</u> when she heard the good news.)

   8. A: I spilled some juice on the floor. _____ ?

      B: Wipe it up with a paper towel. (You <u>should wipe</u> it up with a paper towel.)

9. A: _____ after she graduates?

   B: I think she plans to look for a job in hotel management. (Emily <u>is going to look</u> for a job in hotel management after she graduates.)

10. A: _____ when the fire alarm sounded?

    B: Ran down the stairs and out of the building. (I <u>ran</u> down the stairs and out of the building when the fire alarm sounded.)

11. A: _____ after school today?

    B: Let's go to the shopping mall, okay? (I <u>would like to go</u> to the shopping mall after school today.)

12. A: _____ ?

    B: Make this coin stand on edge. (I'm <u>trying to make</u> this coin stand on edge.)

13. A: _____ ?

    B: He needs to hand in all of his homework. (Kevin <u>needs</u> to hand in all of his homework if he wants to pass advanced algebra.)

14. A: _____ ?

    B: He's an airplane mechanic. (Nick <u>repairs</u> airplanes for a living.)

15. A: Did you say something to that man over there? Why does he look angry?

    B: I accidentally ran into him and stepped on his foot.

    A: _____ ?

    B: Said something nasty. (He <u>said</u> something nasty when I bumped into him.)

    A: _____ ?

    B: Apologized. (I <u>apologized</u>.)

    A: Then _____ ?

    B: Walked away without saying a word. (Then he <u>walked</u> away without saying a word.)

    A: What an unpleasant person!

    B: I didn't mean to step on his foot. It was just an accident.

◇ PRACTICE 14. WHAT KIND OF. (Chart 5-7)
   Directions: Ask questions with ***what kind of***.

   1. A: _____What kind of music_____ do you like best?

      B: Rock 'n roll.

   2. A: _____ do you like to wear?

      B: Jeans and a T-shirt.

   3. A: _____ do you like best?

      B: Fresh fruit and vegetables.

4. A: _____ do you like to read?

   B: Romance novels.

5. A: _____ should I buy?

   B: A four-door sedan with good gas mileage.

6. A: _____ does your country have?

   B: It's a democratic republic.

7. A: _____ would you like to have?

   B: I'd like to have one that pays well, is interesting, and allows me to contribute to society. I've often thought I'd like to be a doctor or an architect.

8. A: _____ would you like to marry?

   B: Someone who is kind-hearted, loving, funny, serious, and steady.

9. A: _____ can we recycle?

   B: Paper, wood, plastic, and aluminum.

◇ **PRACTICE 15. WHICH vs. WHAT. (Chart 5-8)**
   Directions: Complete the questions with *which* or *what*.

   1. A: I have two pens. _____Which_____ one do you want?

      B: That one.

   2. A: I'm hungry.

      B: So am I. _____What_____ are you going to order?

      A: I think I'll have the fish.

   3. A: There are two good movies on TV tonight, a spy movie and a comedy. _____ one do you want to watch?

      B: Let's watch the spy movie.

   4. A: Did you go out last night?

      B: No. I stayed home and watched TV.

      A: _____ did you watch?

      B: A movie.

   5. A: These shoes are comfortable, and so are those shoes. _____ should I buy, these or those? I can't decide.

      B: These.

6. A: There are flights to Atlanta at 7:30 A.M. and 8:40 A.M. _____ one are you

   going to take?

   B: The 7:30 flight.

7. A: _____ does "huge" mean?

   B: "Very big."

8. A: I need some help.

   B: _____ can I do to help?

   A: Please hand me that bowl.

   B: Sure.

9. A: Would you please hand me a sharp knife?

   B: I'd be happy to. There are several in this drawer. _____ one would you like?

   A: That one.

◇ PRACTICE 16. WHO vs. WHOSE. (Chart 5-9)
   Directions: Complete the questions with *who* or *whose*.

   1. A: _____Who_____ is driving to the game tonight?
      B: Heidi is.

   2. A: _____Whose_____ car are we taking to the game?
      B: Heidi's.

   3. A: This notebook is mine. _____ is that? Is it yours?
      B: No, it's Sara's.

   4. A: There's Ms. Adams. _____ is standing next to her?
      B: Mr. Wilson.

   5. A: _____ was the first woman doctor in the United States?
      B: Elizabeth Blackwell, in 1849.

   6. A: Okay. _____ forgot to
      put the ice cream back in the freezer?
      B: I don't know. Don't look at me. It
      wasn't me.

   7. A: _____ motorcycle ran
      into the telephone pole?
      B: Bill's.

   8. A: _____ suitcase did
      you borrow for your trip?
      B: Andy's.

◇ **PRACTICE 17. WHO vs. WHOSE. (Chart 5-9)**
    Directions: Create the questions.

1. A: _____Whose house is that?_____
   B: Pat's. (That's Pat's house.)

2. A: _____Who's living in that house?_____
   B: Pat. (Pat is living in that house.)

3. A: _____
   B: Pedro's. (I borrowed Pedro's umbrella.)

4. A: _____
   B: Linda's. (I used Linda's book.)

5. A: _____
   B: Nick's. (Nick's book is on the table.)

6. A: _____
   B: Nick. (Nick is on the phone.)

7. A: _____
   B: Sue Smith. (That's Sue Smith.) She's a student in my class.

8. A: _____
   B: Sue's. (That's Sue's.) This one is mine.

◇ **PRACTICE 18. Using HOW. (Chart 5-10)**
    Directions: Complete the sentences with any of the words in the list.

busy	*fresh*	*safe*	*soon*
expensive	✓*hot*	*serious*	*well*

1. A: How _____hot_____ does it get in Chicago in the summer?

   B: Very _____hot_____. It can get over 100°. (100°F = 37.8°C)

2. A: How _____ will dinner be ready? I'm really hungry.

   B: In just a few more minutes.

3. A: Look at that beautiful vase! Let's get it.

   B: How _____ is it?

   A: Oh my gosh! Never mind. We can't afford it.

4. A: Sorry to interrupt, Ted, but I need some help. How _____ are you

   today? Do you have time to read over this report?

   B: Well, I'm always _____, but I'll make time to read it.

5. A: How _____ is Toshi about becoming an astronomer?

   B: He's very _____ . He already knows more about the stars and planets than his high school teachers.

6. A: How _____ is a car with an airbag?

   B: Well, there have been bad accidents where both drivers walked away without injuries because of airbags.

7. A: Tomatoes for sale! Hey, lady! Do you want to buy some tomatoes? Tomatoes for sale!

   B: Hmmm. They look pretty good. How _____ are they?

   A: What do you mean "How _____ are they?" Would I sell something that wasn't _____? They were picked from the field just this morning.

8. A: Do you know Jack Young?

   B: Yes.

   A: Oh? How _____ do you know him?

   B: Very _____ . He's one of my closest friends. Why?

   A: He's applied for a job at my store.

◇ **PRACTICE 19. Using HOW FAR, HOW LONG, and HOW OFTEN. (Charts 5-11 → 5-13)**
Directions: Complete the questions with *far*, *long*, or *often*.

1. A: How _____far_____ is it to the nearest police station?
   B: Four blocks.

2. A: How _____long_____ does it take you to get to work?
   B: Forty-five minutes.

3. A: How _____often_____ do you see your family?
   B: Once a week.

4. A: How _____ is it to your office from home?
   B: About twenty miles.

5. A: How _____ is it from here to the airport?
   B: Ten kilometers.

6. A: How _____ do you see your dentist?
   B: Every six months.

7. A: How _____ does it take to get to the airport?
   B: Fifteen minutes.

8. A: How _____ above sea level is Denver, Colorado?
   B: One mile. That's why it's called the Mile High City.

9. A: How _____ does it take to fly from Chicago to Denver?
   B: About three hours.

10. A: How _____ does your department have meetings?
    B: Twice a week.

11. A: How _____ did it take you to build your own boat?
    B: Four years.

12. A: How _____ did you walk?
    B: Two miles.

13. A: How _____ did you walk?
    B: Two hours.

14. A: How _____ does the bus come?
    B: Every two hours.

15. A: How _____ is it from here to the bus stop?
    B: About two blocks.

16. A: How _____ does the ride downtown take?
    B: About 20 minutes.

17. A: How _____ do you take the bus?
    B: Every day.

◇ **PRACTICE 20. Cumulative review. (Charts 5-1 → 5-13)**

Directions: Complete the dialogues by writing questions for the given answers. Use the information in parentheses to form the questions.

1. A: _____What is Jack doing_____?
   B: He's playing tennis. (Jack is playing tennis.)

2. A: _____ with?
   B: Anna. (He is playing tennis with Anna.)

3. A: _____ ?

   B: Serving the ball. (Anna is serving the ball.)

4. A: _____ in the air?

   B: A tennis ball. (She is throwing a tennis ball in the air.)

5. A: _____ ?

   B: Rackets. (Anna and Jack are holding rackets.)

6. A: _____ between them?

   B: A net. (A net is between them.)

7. A: _____ ?

   B: On a tennis court. (They are on a tennis court.)

8. A: _____ ?

   B: For an hour and a half. (They have been playing for an hour and a half.)

9. A: _____ right now?

   B: Jack. (Jack is winning right now.)

10. A: _____ the last game?

    B: Anna. (Anna won the last game.)

◇ PRACTICE 21. Cumulative review. (Charts 5-1 → 5-13)

Directions: Complete the dialogues by writing questions for the given answers. Use the information in parentheses to form the questions.

1. A: ____*When will the clean clothes be*____ dry?

   B: In about an hour. (The clean clothes will be dry in about an hour.)

2. A: _____ Saturday afternoon?

   B: I went to a baseball game. (I went to a baseball game Saturday afternoon.)

3. A: _____ ?

   B: The small paperback. (I bought the small paperback dictionary, not the hardcover one.)

4. A: _____ to clean your apartment before your parents visited?

   B: Four hours. (It took me four hours to clean my apartment before my parents visited.)

5. A: _____ the top shelf?

   B: Stand on a chair. (You can reach the top shelf by standing on a chair.)

6. A: _____ the best?

   B: Whole wheat bread. (I like whole wheat bread the best.)

7. A: _____ the phone when it rang?

   B: Because I was in the middle of dinner with my family. (I didn't answer the phone when it rang because I was in the middle of dinner with my family.)

8. A: _____ to the show with?

   B: Maria and her sister. (I'm going to the show with Maria and her sister.)

9. A: _____ the radio?

   B: Eric. (Eric repaired the radio.)

10. A: _____ in your hometown in the winter?

    B: It's not bad. It rarely gets below zero. (It rarely gets below zero in my hometown in the winter.)

◇ **PRACTICE 22. Tag questions. (Chart 5-16)**
   Directions: Complete the tag questions with the correct verbs.

1. SIMPLE PRESENT

   a. You **like** strong coffee, _____don't_____ you?

   b. David **goes** to Ames High School, _____ he?

   c. Kate and Sara **live** on Tree Road, _____ they?

   d. Jane **has** the keys to storeroom, _____ she?

   e. Jane**'s** in her office, _____ she?

   f. You**'re** a member of this class, _____ you?

   g. Jack **doesn't** have a car, _____ he?

   h. Ann **isn't** from California, _____ she?

2. SIMPLE PAST

   a. Paul **went** to Florida, _____ he?

   b. You **didn't talk** to the boss, _____ you?

   c. Tom's parents **weren't** at home, _____ they?

   d. That **was** Pat's idea, _____ it?

3. PRESENT PROGRESSIVE, *BE GOING TO,* and PAST PROGRESSIVE

   a. You**'re studying** hard, _____ you?

   b. Tom **isn't working** at the bank, _____ he?

   c. It **isn't going to rain** today, _____ it?

   d. Susan and Kevin **were waiting** for us, _____ they?

   e. It **wasn't raining,** _____ it?

4. PRESENT PERFECT

   a. It **has been** warmer than usual, _____ it?

   b. You**'ve had** a lot of homework, _____ you?

c. We **haven't spent** much time together, _____ we?

   d. Lisa **has started** her new job, _____ she?

   e. Bill **hasn't finished** his sales report yet, _____ he?

5. MODAL AUXILIARIES

   a. You **can answer** these questions, _____ you?

   b. Kate **won't tell** anyone our secret, _____ she?

   c. Sam **should come** to the meeting, _____ he?

   d. Alice **would like** to come with us, _____ she?

   e. I **don't have to come** to the meeting, _____ I?

   f. Steve **had to leave** early, _____ he?

◇ PRACTICE 23. Tag questions. (Chart 5-16)
   Directions: Add tag questions to the following and give the expected responses.

   1. A: You've already seen that movie, ___*haven't you?*___

      B: ___*Yes, I have.*___

   2. A: Alex hasn't called, ___*has he?*___

      B: ___*No, he hasn't.*___

   3. A: You talked to Mike last night, ___*didn't you?*___

      B: ___*Yes, I did.*___

   4. A: You usually bring your lunch to school, _____

      B: _____

   5. A: Rita and Philip have been married for five years, _____

      B: _____

   6. A: Kathy has already finished her work, _____

      B: _____

   7. A: This isn't a hard exercise, _____

      B: _____

   8. A: We have to hand in our assignments today, _____

      B: _____

   9. A: Tony Wah lives in Los Angeles, _____

      B: _____

   10. A: You used to live in Los Angeles, _____

       B: _____

11. A: Tomorrow isn't a holiday, _____

    B: _____

12. A: Jack doesn't have to join the army, _____

    B: _____

13. A: I don't have to be at the meeting, _____

    B: _____

14. A: This isn't your book, _____

    B: _____

15. A: Jack and Elizabeth were in class yesterday, _____

    B: _____

16. A: Jennifer won't be here for dinner tonight, _____

    B: _____

◇ PRACTICE 24. Error analysis. (Chapter 5)
Directions: Correct the errors in the sentences.

       Who
1. ~~Whom~~ saw the car accident?

2. Why you didn't say "good-bye" when you left?

3. How about ask Julie and Tim to come for dinner Friday night?

4. What time class begins today?

5. Why he have no shoes on his feet?

6. Where you can get a drink of water in this building?

7. What kind of music you like best?

8. How long it takes to get to the beach from here?

9. She is working late tonight, doesn't she?

10. Who's glasses are those?

11. How much tall your father?

12. Who you talked to about registration for next term?

13. How about we go to see the baby elephant at the zoo tomorrow?

14. How far from here to the nearest gas station?

◇ **PRACTICE 25. Review: questions. (Chapter 5)**
Directions: Using the information in parentheses, complete the questions for the given answers.

1. A: _____When are you going to buy_____ a new bicycle?

   B: Next week. (I'm going to buy a new bicycle next week.)

2. A: _____How are you going to pay_____ for it?

   B: With my credit card. (I'm going to pay for it with my credit card.)

3. A: _____ your old bike?

   B: Ten years. (I had my old bike for ten years.)

4. A: _____ your bike?

   B: Four or five times a week. (I ride my bike four or five times a week.)

5. A: _____ to work?

   B: I usually ride my bike. (I usually get to work by riding my bike.)

6. A: _____ your bike to work tomorrow?

   B: Yes. (I'm going to ride my bike to work tomorrow.)

7. A: _____ your bike to work today?

   B: I decided I would rather walk. (I didn't ride my bike to work today because I decided I would rather walk.)

8. A: _____ a comfortable seat?

   B: Yes, it does. (My bike has a comfortable seat.)

9. A: _____ ?

   B: A ten-speed. (I have a ten-speed bicycle.)

10. A: _____ his new bike?

    B: Two weeks ago. (Jason got his new bike two weeks ago.)

11. A: _____ Jason's new bike?

    B: Billy. (Billy broke Jason's new bike.)

12. A: _____ ?

    B: The front wheel on Jason's new bike. (Billy broke the front wheel on Jason's new bike.)

13. A: _____ ?

    B: Jason's new bike. (Jason's new bike is broken.)

14. A: _____ Jason's bike?

    B: He ran into a brick wall. (Billy broke Jason's bike by running into a brick wall.)

15. A: _____ yours?

    B: The blue one. (The blue bicycle is mine, not the red one.)

16. A: _____ your bicycle at night?

    B: Inside my apartment. (I keep my bicycle inside my apartment at night.)

17. A: _____?

    B: David. (That bike belongs to David.)

18. A: _____?

    B: Suzanne's. (I borrowed Suzanne's bike.)

19. A: _____?

    B: In the park. (Rita is in the park.)

20. A: _____?

    B: Riding her bike. (She's riding her bike.)

21. A: _____ her bike yesterday?

    B: 25 miles. (Rita rode her bike 25 miles* yesterday.)

22. A: _____ "bicycle"?

    B: B-I-C-Y-C-L-E. (You spell "bicycle" B-I-C-Y-C-L-E.)

_____

*25 miles = approximately 40 kilometers/kilometres.

CHAPTER 6
Nouns and Pronouns

◇ PRACTICE 1. Preview: plural nouns. (Chart 6-2)
Directions: Underline each noun. Write the correct plural form if necessary. Do not change any other words.

1. Airplane_^^s have wing_^^s.

2. Child like to play on swing.

3. Some animal live in zoo.

4. Tree grow branch and leaf.

5. I saw three duck and several goose

   in a pond at the park.

6. Some baby are born with a few tooth.

7. I eat a lot of potato, bean, pea, and tomato.

8. Opinion are not the same as fact.

9. Each country has its own custom.

10. Government collect tax.

◇ PRACTICE 2. Pronunciation of -S/-ES. (Chart 6-1)
Directions: Write the correct pronunciations: /s/, /z/, or /əz/. Practice saying the words.

1. dogs = dog + / z /

2. cups = cup + /   /

3. desks = desk + /   /

4. classes = class + /   /

5. doors = door + /   /

6. radios = radio + /   /

7. pages = page + /   /

8. spoons = spoon + /   /

9. sheets = sheet + /   /

10. wishes = wish + /   /

11. collars = collar + /   /

12. shirts = shirt + /   /

◇ PRACTICE 3. Pronunciation of -S/-ES. (Chart 6-1)
Directions: Write the correct pronunciations: /s/, /z/, or /əz/. Practice saying the words.

1. ear / z /

2. cat /   /

3. dish /   /

4. disk /   /

5. table /   /

6. lie /   /

7. letter /   /

8. group /   /

9. nose /   /

10. date /   /

11. purse /   /

12. fox /   /

◇ **PRACTICE 4. Pronunciation of -S/-ES. (Chart 6-1)**

Directions: Write the correct pronunciations for the underlined words: /s/, /z/, or /əz/. Read the sentences aloud.

1. My friends   raise chickens   and cows.
      / z /   /   /   /   /

2. Boxes   come in many different sizes.
    /   /   /   /

3. The doctor checked the child's   eyes,   ears,   and nose.
                                       /   /   /   /   /

4. Most businesses   need to have computers.
          /   /   /   /

5. Apples   and oranges   are my favorite fruits.
    /   /   /   /

6. Sam's   faxes   have several mistakes.
    /   /   /   /   /   /

7. We heard loud voices   from the houses   down the street.
                  /   /   /   /

8. Do you prefer to watch videos   or go to movies   on weekends?
                            /   /   /   /   /   /

◇ **PRACTICE 5. Plural nouns. (Chart 6-2)**

Directions: Write the correct singular or plural form.

	SINGULAR	PLURAL
1.	mouse	mice
2.	pocket	pockets
3.	_____	teeth
4.	_____	tomatoes
5.	_____	fish/fishes
6.	_____	women
7.	branch	_____
8.	friend	_____
9.	duty	_____
10.	highway	_____
11.	thief	thieves
12.	belief	_____

13. potato   _____

14. radio   _____

15. offspring   _____

16. _____   children

17. season   _____

18. custom   _____

19. business   _____

20. _____   centuries

21. occurrence   _____

22. _____   phenomena

23. sheep   _____

24. _____   loaves

25. glass   _____

26. problem   _____

27. family   _____

28. wife   _____

29. shelf   _____

30. roof   _____

31. _____   feet

32. woman   _____

◇ **PRACTICE 6. Plural nouns. (Chart 6-2)**
    Directions: Write the plural of each word from the box in the correct category.

✓ cow	baby	lily	husband	goose
sheep	rose	tomato	pea	child
apple	horse	daughter	cherry	
potato	daisy	strawberry	wife	
poppy	son	mouse	pear	
daffodil	grape	banana	bean	

1. Common farm animals include ____cows,_____ .

2. Common vegetables include _____ .

3. Common fruits include _____ .

4. Common flowers include _____ .

5. Family members include _____ .

◇ **PRACTICE 7. Subjects, verbs, and objects. (Chart 6-3)**

Directions: <u>Underline</u> and identify the subject (**S**) and verb (**V**) of each sentence. Also identify the object (**O**) of the verb if the sentence has an object.

           S   V   O

1. <u>Children</u> <u>play</u> <u>games</u>.

2. Fish swim.

3. The baby doesn't like her new toys.

4. Computers process information quickly.

5. Dictionaries give definitions.

6. Teachers correct tests.

7. The cat found a mouse.

8. The sun shines brightly.

9. Water evaporates.

10. Do snakes lay eggs?

11. The child petted the dog.

12. Did the phone ring?

◇ **PRACTICE 8. Objects of prepositions. (Charts 6-3 and 6-4)**

Directions: <u>Underline</u> and identify the preposition (**PREP**) and object of the preposition (**O of PREP**).

                              PREP O of PREP

1. The man opened the door <u>with</u> his   <u>key</u>.

2. The little girl put her shoes on the wrong feet.

3. The student added and subtracted with a calculator.

4. My father fixes breakfast for my mother every morning.

5. Librarians work in libraries.

6. The bird flew into the window of the building.

7. I do all my homework on a computer.

8. The artist drew scenes of the beach in his notebook.

9. The children played in the backyard until dinner.

10. It rained for two weeks.

11. The painter splashed paint on the floor of his studio.

12. A man with dark glasses stood near the door.

◇ PRACTICE 9. Subjects, verbs, objects, and prepositions. (Charts 6-3 and 6-4)
    Directions: <u>Underline</u> and identify the subjects (**s**), verbs (**v**), objects (**o**), and prepositional phrases (**PP**) in these sentences.

                S   V   O
    1. <u>Bridges</u> <u>cross</u> <u>rivers</u>.

                      S   V   PP
    2. <u>A terrible earthquake</u> <u>occurred</u> <u>in Turkey</u>.

    3. Airplanes fly above the clouds.

    4. Trucks carry large loads.

    5. Rivers flow toward the sea.

    6. Salespeople treat customers with courtesy.

    7. Bacteria can cause diseases.

    8. Clouds are floating across the sky.

    9. The audience in the theater applauded the performers at the end of the show.

   10. Helmets protect bicyclists from serious injuries.

◇ PRACTICE 10. Prepositions of time. (Chart 6-5)
    Directions: Complete the phrases with the correct time prepositions.

The Jacksons got married . . .	**Their baby was born** . . .
1. ___in___ the summer.	9. _____ midnight.
2. _____ June.	10. _____ 12:00 A.M.
3. _____ June 17th.	11. _____ the morning.
4. _____ Saturday.	12. _____ April 12th.
5. _____ 12:00 P.M.	13. _____ 2001.
6. _____ noon.	14. _____ April.
7. _____ 2000.	15. _____ Wednesday.
8. _____ Saturday afternoon.	

◇ PRACTICE 11. Word order: object, place, and time. (Chart 6-6)
   Directions: Complete each sentence by arranging the phrases in the correct order. There is only one correct solution for each sentence.

1. The dog chased   __3__ for several minutes.

                         __1__ a cat

                         __2__ around the room

2. The policeman stopped   _____ the driver

                         _____ at a busy intersection

                         _____ at midnight

3. My friends rented   _____ on the lake

                         _____ last summer

                         _____ a houseboat

4. The children caught   _____ in the river

                         _____ several fish

                         _____ last weekend

5. Our library shows   _____ free movies

                         _____ every Saturday

                         _____ in the children's section

6. We ate   _____ at noon

                         _____ our lunch

                         _____ in the park

7. The little girl always puts   _____ in bed

                         _____ at night

                         _____ her dolls

8. The florist delivers   _____ every Monday

                         _____ fresh flowers

                         _____ to our office

9. I bought   _____ at the corner store

                         _____ a newspaper

                         _____ after work yesterday

◇ PRACTICE 12. Subject–verb agreement. (Chart 6-7)
   Directions: Complete the sentences with **is** or **are**.

   1. These magazines ____*are*____ from the library.

   2. The magazines on the table _____ for you.

   3. Some people _____ wise.

   4. Everyone _____ here.

   5. Everybody _____ on time for class.

   6. Each person in class _____ ready to begin.

   7. Every teacher at this school _____ patient.

   8. There _____ some money on the table.

   9. There _____ some bills for you to pay.

   10. This information about taxes _____ helpful.

◇ PRACTICE 13. Subject–verb agreement. (Chart 6-7)
   Directions: Circle the correct verb.

   1. Bees (*make,*) *makes* honey.

   2. Tomatoes *needs, need* lots of sunshine to grow.

   3. *Do, Does* the people in your neighborhood help each other?

   4. There *is, are* some people already in line for the movie.

   5. The vegetables in the bowl on the table *is, are* fresh.

   6. Everybody always *comes, come* to class on time.

   7. Everyone in the class *is, are* paying attention.

   8. The dishes on the counter *is, are* dirty.

   9. Each person *needs, need* to bring identification.

   10. The people next door *goes, go* hiking every weekend in the summer.

   11. My father and mother *works, work* for the same company.

   12. The pictures on the wall *is, are* of my father's family.

◇ PRACTICE 14. Adjectives. (Chart 6-8)
   Directions: Complete each phrase with an adjective that has the opposite meaning.

   1. new cars   ____*old*____ cars

   2. a young man   an _____ man

   3. a _____ day   a warm day

4. fast trains   _____ trains

5. sad news   _____ news

6. a good day   a _____ day

7. _____ hair   dry hair

8. _____ exercises   hard exercises

9. a soft pillow   a _____ pillow

10. a _____ street   a wide street

11. _____ plates   dirty plates

12. _____ cups   full cups

13. dangerous cities   _____ cities

14. _____ children   quiet children

15. shallow water   _____ water

16. sweet candy   _____ candy

17. _____ clothes   expensive clothes

18. a dark color   a _____ color

19. a heavy box   a _____ box

20. a _____ place   a private place

21. my left foot   my _____ foot

22. the wrong answer   the _____ answer

23. weak coffee   _____ coffee

24. a _____ walk   a short walk

◇ PRACTICE 15. Adjectives and nouns. (Chart 6-8)
Directions: Circle each adjective. Draw an arrow to the noun it describes.

1. Paul has a (loud) voice.

2. Sugar is (sweet.)

3. The students took an easy test.

4. Air is free.

5. We ate some delicious food at a Mexican restaurant.

6. An encyclopedia contains important facts about a wide variety of subjects.

7. The child was sick.

8. The sick child crawled into his warm bed and sipped hot tea.

9. Our camping equipment looks old and rusty.

10. The hungry bear found food in the garbage cans.

11. My elderly father needs nursing care.

12. May I offer you some fresh coffee and warm cookies?

◇ **PRACTICE 16. Nouns as adjectives. (Chart 6-9)**
   Directions: Use the information in *italics* to complete the sentences. Each completion should have a noun that is used as an adjective in front of another noun.

1. *Articles in newspapers* are called ____newspaper articles____.

2. *Numbers on pages* are called _____.

3. *Money that is made of paper* is called _____.

4. *Buildings with apartments* are called _____.

5. *Disks for computers* are called _____.

6. *Presents for birthdays* are called _____.

7. *Gardens with roses* are called _____.

8. *Chains for keys* are called _____.

9. *Governments in cities* are called _____.

10. *Ponds for ducks* are called _____.

11. *Walls made of bricks* are called _____.

12. *Cartons that hold eggs* are called _____.

13. *Views of mountains* are called _____.

14. *Knives that people carry in their pockets* are called _____.

15. *Lights that control traffic* are called _____.

16. *Tables used for outdoor picnics* are called _____.

17. *Pies that are made with apples* are called _____.

18. *Helmets for bicycle riders* are called _____.

19. *Cabins made out of logs* are called _____.

20. *Bridges made from steel* are called _____.

◇ PRACTICE 17. Review: nouns. (Charts 6-2 → 6-9)
Directions: These sentences have many mistakes in the use of nouns. Decide which nouns should be plural and add the correct plural endings to them. Do not change any other words in the sentences.

1. The mountain^s in Chile are beautiful.

2. Cat hunt mouse.

3. Mosquito are small insect.

4. Everyone has eyelash.

5. Goose are larger than duck.

6. What are your favorite radio program?

7. Forest sometimes have fire. Forest fire endanger wild animal.

DUCK

GOOSE

8. Sharp kitchen knife can be dangerous weapon.

9. Good telephone manner are important.

10. I bought two theater ticket for the Thursday evening's performance of *A Doll's House.*

11. Our daily life have changed in many way in the past one hundred year. We no longer need to use oil lamp or candle in our house, raise our own chicken, or build daily fire for cooking.

12. There are approximately 250,000 different kind of flower in the world.

13. Newspaper reporter have high-pressure job.

14. I applied to several foreign university because I want to study abroad next year.

15. Ted lives with three other university student.

16. The offspring of animal like horse, zebra, and deer can run soon after they are born.

17. Science student do laboratory experiment in their class.

18. Housefly are troublesome pest. They carry germ.

19. I like to read magazine article about true personal experience.

20. Many modern device require battery to work. Some flashlight, pocket calculator, portable radio, tape recorder, and many kind of toy need battery.

◇ PRACTICE 18. Personal pronouns. (Chart 6-10)
    Directions: <u>Underline</u> each pronoun. Note how it is used.

- Subject (**s**)
- Object of a verb (**o of v**)
- Object of a preposition (**o of PREP**)

1. The teacher helped <u>me</u> with the lesson.
    (o of v over "me")

2. <u>I</u> carry a dictionary with <u>me</u> at all times.
    (s over "I", o of PREP over "me")

3. Mr. Fong has a computer. He uses it for many things. It helps him in many ways.

4. Jessica went to Hawaii with Ann and me. We like her, and she likes us. We had a good time with her.

5. Mike had dirty socks. He washed them in the kitchen sink and hung them to dry in front of the window. They dried quickly.

6. Joseph and I are close friends. No bad feelings will ever come between him and me. He and I share a strong bond of friendship.

◇ PRACTICE 19. Personal pronouns. (Chart 6-10)
    Directions: Circle each pronoun, then draw an arrow to the noun or noun phrase it refers to. Enclose the noun or noun phrase in brackets.

1. [Janet] had [a green apple.] (She) ate (it) after class.

2. Betsy called this morning. John spoke to her.

3. Nick and Rob are at the market. They are buying fresh vegetables.

4. Eric took some phone messages for Karen. They're on a pad of yellow paper in the kitchen.

5. When Louie called, Alice talked to him. He asked her for a date. She accepted.

6. Jane wrote a letter to Mr. and Mrs. Moore. She mailed it to them yesterday. They should get her letter on Friday.

◇ **PRACTICE 20. Personal pronouns. (Chart 6-10)**
   Directions: Circle the correct pronoun.

   1. You can ride with Jennifer and *I,* (*me.*)

   2. Did you see Mark? *He, Him* was waiting in your office to talk to you.

   3. I saw Rob a few minutes ago. I passed Sara and *he, him* on the steps of the classroom

   building.

   4. Nick used to work in his father's store, but his father and *he, him* had a serious

   disagreement. Nick left and started his own business.

   5. When the doctor came into the room, I asked *she, her* a question.

   6. The doctor was very helpful. *She, Her* answered all of my questions.

   7. Prof. Molina left a message for you and *I, me. He, Him* needs to see *we, us.*

   8. Emily is a good basketball player. I watch Betsy and *she, her* carefully during games.

   They, Them are the best players.

   9. Once my little sister and *I, me* were home alone. When our parents returned, a valuable

   vase was broken. *They, Them* blamed *we, us* for the broken vase, but in truth the cat had

   broken *it, them. We, Us* got in trouble with *they, them* because of the cat.

   10. Take these secret documents and destroy *it, them.*

   11. Ron invited Mary and *I, me* to have dinner with *he, him.*

   12. Maureen likes movies. Ron and *she, her* go to the movies every chance they get.

   13. Tom and *I, me* both want to marry Ann. She has to choose between *he and I, him and me.*

   14. I talked to Jennifer and Mike. I told *they, them* about the surprise birthday party for Lizzy.

   They, Them won't tell *she, her* about *it, them. She, Her* is really going to be surprised!

   15. Ted invited *I, me* to go to the game with *he, him.*

   16. Ted invited Adam and *I, me* to go to the game with Tina and *he, him.*

   17. My brother always teases *I, me* and my sister when *he, him* comes home from college.

   Our parents laugh and tell *he, him* to quit picking on *we, us. We, Us* love the attention.

   We, Us miss *he, him* when *he, him* returns to school.

◇ PRACTICE 21. Possessive nouns. (Chart 6-11)

Directions: Use the *italicized* noun in the first sentence to write a POSSESSIVE NOUN in the second sentence. Pay special attention to where you put the apostrophe.

1. I have one *friend*. My _____friend's_____ name is Paul.

2. I have two *friends*. My _____friends'_____ names are Paul and Kevin.

3. I have one *son*. My _____ name is Ryan.

4. I have two *sons*. My _____ names are Ryan and Scott.

5. I have one *baby*. My _____ name is Joy.

6. I have two *babies*. My _____ names are Joy and Erica.

7. I have one *child*. My _____ name is Anna.

8. I have two *children*. My _____ names are Anna and Keith.

9. I know one *person*. This _____ name is Nick.

10. I know several *people*. These _____ names are Nick, Karen, and Rita.

11. I have one *teacher*. My _____ name is Ms. West.

12. I have two *teachers*. My _____ names are Ms. West and Mr. Fox.

13. I know a *man*. This _____ name is Alan Burns.

14. I know two *men*. These _____ names are Alan Burns and Joe Lee.

15. We live on the *earth*. The _____ surface is seventy percent water.

◇ PRACTICE 22. Possessive nouns. (Chart 6-11)

Directions: Make the nouns possessive if necessary.

1. I met ~~Dan~~ Dan's sister yesterday.

2. I met Dan and his sister yesterday. OK *(no change)*

3. I know Jack roommates.

4. I know Jack well. He's a good friend of mine.

5. I have one roommate. My roommate desk is always messy.

6. You have two roommates. Your roommates desks are always neat.

7. Jo Ann and Betty are sisters.

8. Jo Ann is Betty sister. My sister name is Sonya.

9. My name is Richard. I have two sisters. My sisters names are Jo Ann and Betty.

10. There is an old saying: "A woman work is never done."

11. I read a book about the changes in women roles and men roles in modern society.

12. Jupiter is the largest planet in our solar system. We cannot see Jupiter surface from the earth because thick clouds surround the planet.

13. Mercury is the closest planet to the sun. Mercury atmosphere is extremely hot and dry.

14. Mars* surface has some of the same characteristics as Earth surface, but Mars could not support life as we know it on Earth. The plants and animals that live on Earth could not live on any of the other planets in our solar system.

15. Venus is sometimes called Earth twin because the two planets are almost the same size. But like Mars, Venus surface is extremely hot and dry.

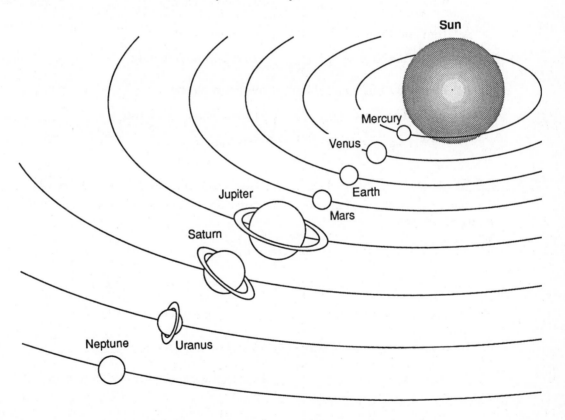

---

*When a singular noun ends in -s, there are two possible possessive forms, as in the examples below:

SINGULAR NOUNS	POSSESSIVE FORMS
James	I know *James'* brother. OR I know *James's* brother.
Chris	*Chris'* car is red. OR *Chris's* car is red.
Carlos	*Carlos'* last name is Rivera. OR *Carlos's* last name is Rivera.

16. The planets English names come from ancient Roman mythology. For example, Mars was

the name of the god of war in ancient Rome. Jupiter was the king of the gods. Mercury, who

was Jupiter son, was the messenger of the gods. Venus was the goddess of love, beauty, and

creativity. Venus son was named Cupid, the god of love and desire.

◇ **PRACTICE 23. Possessive pronouns vs. possessive adjectives. (Chart 6-12)**
Directions: Complete the sentences with possessive pronouns or possessive adjectives that refer to the words in *italics*.

1. A: Can I look at your grammar book?

    B: Why? *You* have _____your_____ own* book. *You* have _____yours_____, and I have mine.

2. A: Anna wants to look at your grammar book.

    B: Why? *She* has _____ own book. *She* has _____, and I have mine.

3. A: Tom wants to look at your grammar book.

    B: Why? *He* has _____ own book. *He* has _____, and I have mine.

4. A: Tom and I want to look at your grammar book.

    B: Why? *You* have _____ own books. *You* have _____, and I have mine.

5. A: Tom and Anna want to look at our grammar books.

    B: Why? *They* have _____ own books. *We* have _____ own books. *They*
    have _____, and *we* have _____.

◇ **PRACTICE 24. Possessive pronouns vs. possessive adjectives. (Chart 6-12)**
Directions: Complete the sentences with possessive pronouns or possessive adjectives that refer to the words in *italics*.

1. *Sara* asked _____her_____ mother for permission to go to a movie.

2. I don't need to borrow your bicycle. *Sara* loaned me _____hers_____.

3. *Ted and I* are roommates. _____ apartment is small.

4. Brian and Louie have a huge apartment, but *we* don't. _____ is small.

5. *You* can find _____ keys in the top drawer of the desk.

***Own** frequently follows a possessive adjective: e.g., *my own, your own, their own.* The word **own** emphasizes that nobody else
possesses the exact same thing(s); ownership belongs **only** to me *(my own book)*, to you *(your own book)*, to them *(their own
books)*, to us *(our own books)*, etc.

6. The keys in the drawer belong to you. *I* have _____ in _____ pocket.

   You should look in the drawer for _____ .

7. *Tom and Paul* talked about _____ experiences in the wilderness areas of

   Canada. I've had a lot of interesting experiences in the wilderness, but nothing to compare

   with _____ .

8. *I* know Eric well. He is a good friend of _____ . *You* know him, too, don't you?

   Isn't he a friend of _____ , too?

9. Omar, *my wife and I* would like to introduce you to a good friend of _____ .

   His name is Dan Lightfeather.

◇ PRACTICE 25. Reflexive pronouns. (Chart 6-13)
   Directions: Complete the sentences with reflexive pronouns that refer to the words in *italics*.

1. *I* enjoyed _____myself_____ at Disney World.

2. *Paul* enjoyed _____ .

3. *Paul and I* enjoyed _____ .

4. Hi, Emily! Did *you* enjoy _____ ?

5. Hi, Emily and Dan! Did *you* enjoy _____ ?

6. *Jessica* enjoyed _____ .

7. *Jessica and Paul* enjoyed _____ .

8. *Joe* helped _____ to more dessert.

9. *Jane* helped _____ .

10. *I* helped _____ .

11. *We* helped _____ .

12. *They* helped _____ .

13. *The new teacher* introduced _____ to the students.

14. *My friends and I* introduced _____ .

15. *The assistant teacher and school nurse* introduced _____ .

16. *Ann* introduced _____ .

17. *Jack* introduced _____.

18. *The other teachers* introduced _____.

19. Did *you* introduce _____?

◇ **PRACTICE 26. Reflexive pronouns.** (Chart 6-13)

Directions: Choose an expression and complete the sentences. Be sure to use the correct reflexive pronoun.

be proud of	help	talk to
blame	introduce	teach
✓ cut	take care of	work for
enjoy		

1. Ouch! I just _____ cut myself _____ with a knife.

2. You graduated with top honors in your class. Congratulations, Anna! You must _____

   _____ .

3. John often _____ . People think there is more than one person

   in the room, but there isn't. It's only John.

4. When I was young, I _____ to ride a bicycle. Then I taught

   the other children in the neighborhood.

5. Sheri _____ for the accident, but it wasn't her fault. There was

   nothing she could have done when the car came toward her.

6. Eat! Eat! There's lots more pizza in the oven. Please, all of you, _____

   _____ .

7. Adam seldom gets sick because he eats nourishing food and exercises regularly. He

   _____ .

8. They went to a party last night. Let's ask them if they _____ .

9. My father never worked for anyone. He always owned his own company. He _____

   _____ throughout his entire adult life.

10. At the beginning of each term, my students walk around the room and greet each other.

    When they finish, they _____ to the

    whole class.

◇ PRACTICE 27. Review: pronouns. (Charts 6-10 → 6-13)
   Directions: Circle the correct pronouns.

1. Nick invited   *I,* (me) to go to dinner with   *he,* (him.)

2. Sam and you should be proud of   *yourself, yourselves.* The two of you did a good job.

3. The room was almost empty. The only furniture was one table. The table stood by   *it, itself*

   in one corner.

4. The bird returned to   *its, it's** nest to feed   *its, it's*   offspring.

5. Nick has his tennis racket, and Ann has   *her, hers, her's.**

6. Where's Eric? I have some good news for Joe and   *he, him, his, himself.*

7. Don't listen to Greg. You need to think for   *yourself, yourselves,*   Jane. It's

   you, your, your's*   life.

8. We all have   *us, our, ours*   own ideas about how to live   *our, ours, our's**   lives.

9. You have your beliefs, and we have   *our, ours.*

10. People usually enjoy   *themself, themselves, theirselves***   at family gatherings.

11. History repeats   *himself, herself, itself.*

12. David didn't need my help. He finished the work by   *him, himself, his, his self.*

◇ PRACTICE 28. Review: pronouns. (Charts 6-10 → 6-13)
   Directions: Complete the sentences with pronouns that refer to the words in *italics*.

1. *Tom* is wearing a bandage on _____his_____ arm. _____He_____ hurt _____himself_____

   while _____he_____ was repairing the roof. I'll help _____him_____ with the roof later.

2. I have *a sister.* _____ name is Kate. _____ and I share a room.

3. *My sister and I* share a room. _____ room is pretty small. _____ have

   only one desk.

4. Our desk has five drawers. *Kate* puts _____ things in the two drawers on the right.

_____

*REMINDER: Apostrophes are NOT used with possessive pronouns. Note that ***its*** = possessive adjective; ***it's*** = *it is.* Also note that *her's, your's,* and *our's* are NOT POSSIBLE in grammatically correct English.

NOTE: *Themself and theirselves* are not really words—they are NOT POSSIBLE in grammatically correct English. Only ***themselves* is the correct reflexive pronoun form.

5. *I* keep _____ stuff in the two drawers on the left. She and _____ share the middle drawer.

6. *Kate* doesn't open my two drawers, and I don't open _____ .

7. *I* don't put things in her drawers, and she doesn't put things in _____ .

8. *Ms. Lake and Mr. Ramirez* work together at the advertising company. _____ often work on projects by _____ , but I work with _____ sometimes. My office is next to _____ . _____ office has _____ names on the door, and mine has my name.

9. I have my dictionary, and *Sara* has _____ . But *Nick* doesn't have _____ .

10. My friend *James* enjoyed _____ at Mike's house yesterday. When I talked to _____ on the phone, _____ told me about _____ day with Mike. _____ and Mike played basketball, ate junk food, and played computer games. I like James a lot. I'm going to spend next Saturday with Mike and _____ at a science fair.

11. *Karen* has a bandage on _____ thumb because _____ accidentally cut _____ with a hatchet while _____ was cutting wood for _____ fireplace.

12. We don't agree with you. *You* have _____ opinion, and *we* have _____ .

◇ PRACTICE 29. Singular forms of OTHER. (Chart 6-14)
Directions: Write *another* or *the other* under each picture.

1. Four boxes: __one__   __another__   __another__   __the other__

2. Three circles: __one__   _____   _____

3. Five flowers: __one__ _____ _____ _____ _____

4. Two cups: __one__ _____

5. Six spoons: __one__ _____ _____ _____ _____ _____

◇ **PRACTICE 30. Singular forms of OTHER. (Chart 6-14)**
   Directions: Complete the sentences with ***another*** or ***the other***.

   1. There are many kinds of animals in the world. The elephant is one kind. The tiger is

      _____another_____ .

   2. There are two colors on this page. One is white. _____The other_____ is black.

   3. There are two women in Picture A. One is Ann. _____ is Sara.

   4. There are three men in Picture B. One is Alex. _____ one is Mike.

   5. In Picture B, Alex and Mike are smiling. _____ man looks sad.

   6. There are three men in Picture B. All three have common first names. One is named Alex.

      a. _____ is named David.

      b. The name of _____ one is Mike.

7. There are many common English names for men. Alex is one.

    a. Mike is _____ .

    b. David is _____ .

    c. John is _____ common name.

    d. Joe is _____ .

    e. What is _____ common English name for a man?

8. Alex's bicycle was run over by a truck and destroyed. He needs to get _____ one.

9. The Smiths have two bicycles. One belongs to Mr. Smith. _____ bike belongs to Mrs. Smith.

10. There are three books on my desk. Two of them are dictionaries. _____ one is a telephone directory.

11. The puppy chewed up my telephone directory, so I went to the telephone company to get _____ phone book.

◇ **PRACTICE 31. Plural forms of OTHER. (Chart 6-15)**
Directions: Complete the sentences with *the other, the others, other,* or *others*.

1. There are four common nicknames for "Robert." One is "Bob." Another is "Bobby."
   _____The others_____ are "Robbie" and "Rob."

2. There are five English vowels. One is "a." Another is "e." _____ are "i," "o," and "u."

3. There are many consonants in English. The letters "b" and "c" are consonants. _____ are "d," "f," and "g."

4. Some people are tall, and _____ are short. Some people are neither tall nor short.

5. Some people are tall, and _____ people are short.

6. Some animals are huge. _____ are tiny.

7. Some animals are huge. _____ animals are tiny.

8. Some ships are fueled by petroleum. _____ are propelled by atomic power.

9. Some boats are used for pleasure. _____ boats are used for commercial fishing.

10. Of the twenty students in the class, eighteen passed the exam. _____

    failed.

11. Out of the twenty students in the class, only two failed the exam. _____

    students passed.

12. Our physical education class was divided into two groups. Half of the students stayed inside

    and played basketball. _____ students went outside and played soccer.

13. The telephone and the automobile are twentieth-century inventions. _____

    are the computer, television, and the airplane. Can you name _____

    twentieth-century inventions?

14. If you really hate your job, why don't you look for _____ one? You don't

    have to be a dishwasher all your life. There are lots of _____ jobs in the

    world.

15. An automobile consists of many parts. The motor is one, and the steering wheel is

    _____ . _____ parts are the brakes, the trunk, and

    the fuel tank.

16. The students in our class had two choices: basketball or soccer. Half of the students played

    basketball. _____ played soccer.

17. Here, children. I have two coins. One is for you, Tommy. _____ is for

    you, Jimmy.

◇ PRACTICE 32. Summary: forms of OTHER. (Charts 6-14 → 6-16)
   Directions: Choose the correct completion.

   Example: Copper is one kind of metal. Silver is _____ .
      (A.) another   B. the other   C. the others   D. others   E. other

   1. Summer is one season. Spring is _____ .
      A. another   B. the other   C. the others   D. others   E. other

   2. There are four seasons. Summer is one. _____ are winter, fall, and spring.
      A. Another   B. The other   C. The others   D. Others   E. Other

   3. What's your favorite season? Some people like spring the best. _____ think fall is the nicest
      season.
      A. Another   B. The other   C. The others   D. Others   E. Other

   4. My eyes are different colors. One eye is gray, and _____ is green.
      A. another   B. the other   C. the others   D. others   E. other

5. There are two reasons not to buy that piece of furniture. One is that it's expensive. _____ is that it's not well made.
   A. Another   B. The other   C. The others   D. Others   E. Other

6. Alex failed his English exam, but his teacher is going to give him _____ chance to pass it.
   A. another   B. the other   C. the others   D. others   E. other

7. Some people drink tea in the morning. _____ have coffee. I prefer fruit juice.
   A. Another   B. The other   C. The others   D. Others   E. Other

8. There are five digits in the number 20,000. One digit is a 2. _____ digits are all zeroes.
   A. Another   B. The other   C. The others   D. Others   E. Other

◇ PRACTICE 33. Cumulative review. (Chapter 6)
Directions: Circle the correct answer.

1. The people at the market   *is,* *(are)*   friendly.

2. How many   *potato,* *potatoes*   should I cook for dinner tonight?

3. I wanted to be alone, so I worked   *myself,* *by myself.*

4. The twins were born   *in,* *on*   December 25   *on,* *at*   midnight.

5. All the workers at our company get   *four-week,* *four-weeks*   vacations.

6. The bus driver waited for   *we,* *us*   at the bus stop.

7. Can you tell a good book by   *its,* *it's*   title?

8. This is   *our,* *ours*   dessert, and that is   *your,* *yours.*

9. Jack has so much confidence. He really believes in   *him,* *himself.*

10. These bananas are OK, but   *the other,* *the others*   were better.

◇ PRACTICE 34. Cumulative review. (Chapter 6)
Directions: Correct the errors.

1. Look at those beautifuls mountains!

2. The children played on Saturday afternoon at the park a game.

3. There are two horse, several sheeps, and a cow in the farmers field.

4. The owner of the store is busy in the moment.

5. The teacher met her's students at the park after school.

6. Everyone want peace in the world.

7. I grew up in a city very large.

8. This apple tastes sour. Here's some more, so let's try the other one.

9. Some tree lose their leaf in the winter.

10. I am going to wear my shirt is brown to the party.

11. I hurt meself at work last week.

12. Our neighbors invited my friend and I to visit they.

13. My husband boss works for twelve hour every days.

14. The students couldn't find they're books.

15. I always read magazines articles while I'm in the waiting room at my dentists office.

CHAPTER 7
Modal Auxiliaries

◇ PRACTICE 1. Preview: modal auxiliaries. (Chapter 7)

Directions: The words in **boldfaced italics** are modal auxiliaries. Read the passage and then answer the questions.

(1)   Everyone in my family **has to** contribute to keeping order in our house. My parents

(2)   assign chores to my brother Joe and me. We **must** do these tasks every day. Sometimes if

(3)   one of us is busy and **can't** do a chore, the other one **may** take care of it.

(4)   For example, last Friday it was Joe's turn to wash the dishes after dinner. He said he

(5)   **couldn't** wash them because he had to hurry to school for a basketball game. Joe asked me,

(6)   "**Will** you do the dishes for me, please? I promise to do them for you tomorrow when it's

(7)   your turn. I**'ve got to** get to school for the game." I reluctantly agreed to do Joe's chore

(8)   and washed the dishes after dinner.

(9)   But the next night, Joe "forgot" that we had traded days. When I reminded him to

(10)   wash the dishes, he said, "Who, me? It's not my turn. You **have to** do the dishes tonight.

(11)   It's your turn."

(12)   I think I**'d better** write our agreement down when I do my brother Joe's chores, and I

(13)   **ought to** give him a copy of the agreement. Joe has a short memory, especially if he **has to**

(14)   wash dishes or take out the

(15)   garbage. I **should** write

(16)   everything down. In fact, I

(17)   **might** write out a weekly

(18)   schedule. Then, we **could**

(19)   write our names in and change

(20)   assignments if necessary. That

(21)   **ought to** solve the problem.

(22)   I **must** remember to do that.

What is the meaning of these modal auxiliaries from the sentences in the passage? Circle the answer that is closest in meaning to the modal.

	MODAL AUXILIARY		MEANING		
(1)	Everyone *has to* contribute	(must)	should	is able to	might
(3)	. . . and *can't* do a chore	must not	should not	is not able to	might not
(3)	. . . the other one *may* take care of it.	must	should	is able to	might
(5)	He *couldn't* wash them	must not	should not	was not able to	might not
(7)	I've *got to* get to school	must	should	are able to	might
(10)	You *have to* do the dishes	must	should	are able to	might
(12)	I think *I'd better* write	must	should	am able to	might
(13)	. . . and I *ought to* give him	must	should	am able to	may
(13)	. . . especially if he *has to*	must	should	is able to	may
(17)	In fact, I *might* write out	must	should	am able to	may
(21)	. . . That *ought to* solve the problem.	must	should	is able to	may

◇ PRACTICE 2. The form of modal auxiliaries. (Chart 7-1)
   Directions: Add the word *to* where necessary. Write Ø if *to* is not necessary.

1. Mr. Alvarez spilled tea on his shirt. He must ____Ø____ change clothes before dinner.

2. Mr. Alvarez has ____to____ change his shirt before dinner.

3. Tom and I might _____ play tennis after work tomorrow.

4. You had better _____ see a doctor.

5. Would you _____ speak more slowly, please?

6. The students have _____ take a test next Friday.

7. Everyone should _____ pay attention to local politics.

8. Everyone ought _____ participate in local government.

9. May I please _____ have the salt and pepper? Thanks.

10. You'd better not _____ come to the meeting late. The boss will _____ be angry if you're late.

11. I've had a lot of trouble sleeping the last few nights. I've got _____ get a good night's sleep! I can barely _____ stay awake in class.

12. We may _____ go to Argentina for our vacation.

13. Will you please _____ mail this letter for me?

◇ **PRACTICE 3. Expressing ability. (Chart 7-2)**
   Directions: Choose one of the words in parentheses to complete each sentence.

1. *(giraffe, zebra)*   A ___zebra___ **can't stretch** its neck to reach the tops of trees.

2. *(bee, cat)*   A single _____ **can kill** a thousand mice in a year.

3. *(Rabbits, Elephants)*   _____ **can crush** small trees under their huge feet.

4. *(Monkeys, Chickens)*   _____ **can climb** trees with ease.

5. *(ducks, camels)*   Did you know that _____ **can survive** seventeen days
   without any water at all?

6. *(cow, bull)*   One _____ **can produce** as much as 8,500 lbs. (3,860 kgs)
   of milk in a year.

7. *(horse, cat)*   A person **can sit** on a _____ without hurting it.

8. *(donkey, snake)*   A _____ **can carry** heavy loads on its back.

9. *(squirrel, polar bear)*   A _____ **can stay** high up in the trees for weeks,
   leaping from branch to branch.

10. *(people, ants)*   Most _____ **can lift** objects that are ten times heavier
    than their own bodies.

11. *(baby, student)*   When I was a _____ , I **could sleep** most of the day.

12. *(men, women)*   One hundred years ago, _____ **couldn't vote** in many
    countries, but now they can.

◇ **PRACTICE 4. Expressing ability and possibility. (Charts 7-2 and 7-3)**
   Directions: Complete the sentences with *can/can't*, *may/might*, or *may not/might not*.

1. Jessica hasn't made up her mind about where to go to school. She ___may/might___
   attend Duke University, or she ___may not/might not___ . She just doesn't know yet.

2. Alice is a runner. She likes to compete, but two days ago she broke her ankle when she fell.
   She ___can't___ run in the race tomorrow.

3. A: Carol's in New York now. Is she going to return to school in Chicago in September?

   B: It depends. If she _____ find a job in New York, she'll stay there
   this fall. Who knows? She _____ stay there through the winter
   and spring, too. If she likes her job, she _____ want to return to
   school in Chicago next year at all. We'll have to wait and see.

4. A: Do you remember a famous actor named Basil Rathbone? Is he still making movies?

   B: I think he _____ be dead.

5. Jodie finished law school last month, but she hasn't taken her exams yet. She

   _____ practice law until she passes them.

6. Jack and Jenny haven't decided what kind of wedding to have. They _____

   have a large, formal celebration, or they _____ have a small, quiet

   ceremony.

7. My roommate is planning to go sailing tomorrow, but he needs at least one other person to

   help him sail the boat. If no one is available, he _____ take it out.

◇ PRACTICE 5. Expressing possibility. (Chart 7-3)
   Directions: Rewrite the sentences using the words in parentheses.

   1. Maybe I will take a nap. *(might)* → ____I might take a nap.____

   2. She might be sick. *(maybe)* → ____Maybe she is sick.____

   3. There may be time later. *(maybe)* → _____

   4. Maybe our team will win. *(may)* → _____

   5. You may be right. *(might)* → _____

   6. Maybe we'll hear soon. *(may)* → _____

   7. It might rain. *(may)* → _____

   8. Maybe it will snow. *(might)* → _____

   9. She might come tomorrow. *(maybe)* → _____

   10. She might be at home right now. *(maybe)* → _____

◇ PRACTICE 6. Expressing possibility and permission. (Chart 7-3)
   Directions: Decide if the meaning of the modal verb is *possibility* or *permission*.

MODAL VERB	MEANING

1. Both of my grandparents are retired. They like to travel.

   They ***may travel*** overseas next summer.   (possibility)   *permission*

2. They ***may take*** their two grandchildren with them.   *possibility*   *permission*

3. A: Yes, Tommy, you ***may play*** outdoors until dinner.   *possibility*   *permission*

   B: Okay, Mom.

4. A: What's wrong with the dog's foot?

   B: He ***may have*** an infection.   *possibility*   *permission*

	MODAL VERB	**MEANING**	

5. The dog has an infected foot. He **might need** to go to the vet.   *possibility*   *permission*

6. A: Susie, no, you **can't stay** overnight at your friend's   *possibility*   *permission*
   house tonight.

   B: Then how about my friend staying overnight here?

   A: No.

7. It **may be** hot and humid all weekend.   *possibility*   *permission*

8. Johnny, you **may not stay** up until midnight. Your   *possibility*   *permission*
   bedtime is nine o'clock.

9. I **might not stay** up to watch the end of the game on   *possibility*   *permission*
   TV. I'm sleepy.

10. Children, you **cannot go** out now. It's dark outside, and   *possibility*   *permission*
    dinner is ready.

◇ PRACTICE 7. Meanings of COULD. (Charts 7-2 and 7-4)
   Directions: Choose the expression that has the same meaning as the *italicized* verb.

1. "How long will it take you to paint two small rooms?"
   "I'm not sure. If the job is not complicated, I *could finish* by Thursday."
   a. was able to finish   (b.) might finish

2. I think I'll take my umbrella. It *could rain* today.
   a. was able to rain   b. might rain

3. My niece *could read* by the time she was four years old.
   a. was able to read   b. might read

4. You *could see* that the little boy was unhappy because of the sad expression in his eyes.
   a. were able to see   b. might see

5. Sally is in excellent condition. I think she *could win* the 10-kilometer race on Saturday.
   a. was able to win   b. might win

6. John *couldn't drive* for a month because of a broken ankle, but now it's healed.
   a. wasn't able to drive   b. might not drive

7. Jane *could arrive* before dinner, but I don't really expect her until nine or later.
   a. was able to arrive   b. might arrive

8. John was in an accident, but he *couldn't remember* how he had hurt himself.
   a. wasn't able to remember   b. might not remember

◇ PRACTICE 8. Polite questions. (Charts 7-5 and 7-6)
    Directions: Circle the correct completion.

1. A: This desk is too heavy for me. *May,* (*Can*) you help me lift it?
   B: Sure. No problem.

2. A: Ms. Milano, *may, will* I be excused from class early today? I have a doctor's appointment.
   B: Yes. You may leave early. That would be fine.

3. A: I'm having trouble with this word processor. *Would, May* you show me how to set the margins one more time?
   B: Of course.

4. A: Andrew, *would, could* I speak to you for a minute?
   B: Sure. What's up?

5. A: I can't meet David's plane tonight. *Can, May* you pick him up?
   B: Sorry. I have to work tonight. Call Uncle Frank. Maybe he can pick David up.

6. A: *Could, May* you please take these letters to the post office before noon?
   B: I'd be happy to, sir. Hmmm. It's almost eleven-thirty. *May, Will* I leave for the post office now and then go to lunch early?
   A: That would be fine.

7. A: Marilyn, are you feeling okay? *Would, Can* I get you something?
   B: *May, Will* you get me a glass of water, please?
   A: Right away.

8. A: Darn these medicine bottles! I can never get the cap off!
   B: *Would, Could* I open that for you?
   A: Thanks. I'd really appreciate it.

◇ PRACTICE 9. Polite questions. (Charts 7-5 and 7-6)
    Directions: Check all the modal auxiliaries that correctly complete each question.

1. It's cold in here. _____ you please close the door?
   _____ May   ✓ Could   ✓ Can   ✓ Would

2. Oh, my pen's out of ink. _____ I borrow yours?
   _____ Could   _____ May   _____ Will   _____ Can

3. I can't lift this box by myself. _____ you help me carry it?
   _____ Would   _____ Could   _____ May   _____ Will

4. Hello. _____ I help you find something in the store?
   _____ Can   _____ Would   _____ May   _____ Could

5. The store closes in ten minutes. _____ you please bring all your purchases to the counter?
   _____ Will   _____ May   _____ Can   _____ Could

◇ **PRACTICE 10. Expressing advice.** (Chart 7-7)

Directions: Complete the sentences. Use **should** or **shouldn't** and the expressions in the list or your own words.

be cruel to animals	give too much homework
always be on time for an appointment	miss any classes
✓drive a long distance	quit
exceed the speed limit	throw trash out of your car window

1. If you are tired, you ___shouldn't drive a long distance___.

2. Cigarette smoking is dangerous to your health. You _____.

3. A good driver _____.

4. A teacher _____.

5. A student _____.

6. Animals have feelings, too. You _____
   _____.

7. It is important to be punctual. You
   _____
   _____.

8. Littering is against the law. You
   _____
   _____
   _____.

NO LITTERING $300 Fine

◇ **PRACTICE 11. Expressing advice.** (Chart 7-7)

Directions: Choose the completion from the given list that seems best to you.

call the landlord and complain	✓soak it in cold water
eat it	take it back to the store
find a new girlfriend	try to fix it herself
get a job	✓wash it in hot water
send it back to the kitchen	

1. A: I cut my finger. I got blood on my shirt. My finger is okay, but I'm worried about my shirt. What should I do?

   B: You should ___soak it in cold water___.

   You shouldn't ___wash it in hot water___.

2. A: Ann bought a new tape recorder. After two days, it stopped working. What should she do?

   B: She ought to _____.

   She shouldn't _____.

3. A: I don't have any money. I'm broke and can't pay my rent. I don't have enough money to pay my bills. What should I do?

B: You'd better _____.

4. A: There's no hot water in my apartment. What should I do?

B: You should _____.

5. A: I asked Mary to marry me five times. She said no every time. What should I do?

B: Maybe you should _____.

6. A: Helen is in a restaurant. She has ordered a salad. There's a big dead fly in it. What should she do?

B: She should _____.

She shouldn't _____.

◇ PRACTICE 12. Expressing advice. (Charts 7-7 and 7-8)
Directions: Choose the correct completion.

1. Danny doesn't feel well. He _____ see a doctor.
   (A.) should   B. ought   C. had

2. Danny doesn't feel well. He _____ better see a doctor.
   A. should   B. ought   C. had

3. Danny doesn't feel well. He _____ to see a doctor.
   A. should   B. ought   C. had

4. It's extremely warm in here. We _____ open some windows.
   A. should   B. ought   C. had

5. It's really cold in here. We _____ to close some windows.
   A. should   B. ought   C. had

6. There's a police car behind us. You _____ better slow down!
   A. should   B. ought   C. had

7. People who use public parks _____ clean up after themselves.
   A. should   B. ought   C. had

8. I have no money left in my bank account. I _____ better stop charging things on my credit card.
   A. should   B. ought   C. had

9. It's going to be a formal dinner and dance. You _____ to change clothes.
   A. should   B. ought   C. had

10. This library book is overdue. I _____ better return it today.
    A. should   B. ought   C. had

◇ PRACTICE 13. Expressing necessity. (Chart 7-9)
   Directions: Choose the correct completion.

1. I _____ to wash the dishes after dinner last night. It was my turn.
   A. have   B. has   C. had   D. must

2. Bye! I'm leaving now. I _____ got to take this package to the post office.
   A. have   B. has   C. had   D. must

3. I know you didn't mean what you said. You _____ think before you speak!
   A. have   B. has   C. had   D. must

4. Yesterday everyone in the office _____ to leave the building for a fire drill. I'm glad it wasn't a real fire.
   A. have   B. has   C. had   D. must

5. Janet _____ to take an educational psychology course next semester. It's a required course.
   A. have   B. has   C. had   D. must

6. Pete, Chris, and Anna _____ to stay after class this afternoon. Professor Irwin wants them to help him grade papers.
   A. have   B. has   C. had   D. must

7. Mr. Silva, you _____ not be late today. The vice-president is coming in, and you're the only one who can answer her questions about the new project.
   A. have   B. has   C. had   D. must

8. Last year our town didn't have many tourists because of an oil spill. Business was bad. My wife and I own a small souvenir shop near the ocean. We _____ to borrow money from the bank last month to save our business.
   A. have   B. has   C. had   D. must

◇ PRACTICE 14. Expressing necessity. (Chart 7-9)
   Directions: Complete the sentences with any appropriate forms of **have to** and **must**.

1. I can't go to the movie tonight because I ___*have to/must*___ study for final exams.

2. When I was in high school, I _____ work every evening at my parents' store.

3. If you want to travel to certain countries, you _____ get a visa.

4. I'm sorry I was absent from class yesterday, but I _____ go to a funeral.

5. Erica won't be in her office tomorrow afternoon because she _____ pick her brother up at the airport.

6. When I worked in my uncle's restaurant, I _____ wash dishes and clear tables.

7. If you want to enter the university, you _____ take an entrance exam.

8. We wanted to go bike riding along the river yesterday, but we _____ stay home because the weather was awful.

◇ PRACTICE 15. Necessity: MUST, HAVE TO, HAVE GOT TO. (Chart 7-9)
   Directions: Circle the correct verb.

   1. Last week, John   *must,* (had to) interview five people for the new management position.

   2. Professor Drake   *had got to, had to*   cancel several lectures when she became ill.

   3. Why did you   *have to, had to*   leave work early ?

   4. I   *must, had to*   take my daughter to the airport yesterday.

   5. Where did John   *have to, had to*   go for medical help yesterday?

   6. We   *had to, had got to*   contact a lawyer last week about a problem with our neighbors.

◇ PRACTICE 16. Necessity: MUST, HAVE TO, HAVE GOT TO. (Chart 7-9)
   Directions: Write the past tense of the verb in *italics.*

   1. I *have to study* for my medical school exams.

      PAST: I ____had to study____ for my medical school exams.

   2. We *have to turn off* our water because of a leak.

      PAST: We _____ our water because of a leak.

   3. *Do you have to work* over the holidays?

      PAST: _____ you _____ over the holidays?

   4. Jerry *has got to see* the dentist twice this week.

      PAST: Jerry _____ the dentist twice last month.

   5. Who *has got to be* in early for work this week?

      PAST: Who _____ in early for work last week?

   6. The bank *must close* early today.

      PAST: The bank _____ early yesterday.

◇ PRACTICE 17. Expressing lack of necessity and prohibition. (Chart 7-10)
   Directions: Complete the sentences with ***don't/doesn't have to*** or ***must not***.

   1. The soup is too hot. You ____must not____ eat it yet. Wait for it to cool.

   2. You ____don't have to____ have soup for lunch. You can have a sandwich if you like.

   3. The review class before the final exam is optional. We _____ go
      unless we want to.

   4. Many vegetables can be eaten raw. You _____ cook them.

   5. You _____ use a pencil to write a check because someone could
      change the amount you have written on it.

6. When the phone rings, you _____ answer it. It's up to you.

7. When you have a new job, you _____ be late the first day. In fact, it is a good idea to be a few minutes early.

8. A: I _____ forget to set my alarm for 5:30.

   B: Why do you have to get up at 5:30?

   A: I'm going to meet Ron at 6:00. We're going fishing.

9. You _____ play loud music late at night. The neighbors will call the police.

10. This box isn't as heavy as it looks. You _____ help me with it. Thanks anyway for offering to help.

11. Susan, you _____ go to the university. Your father and I think you should, but it's your choice.

12. People _____ spend their money foolishly if they want to stay out of financial trouble.

13. When you first meet someone, you _____ ask personal questions. For example, it's not polite to ask a person's age.

14. The nations of the world _____ stop trying to achieve total world peace.

15. My husband and I grow all of our own vegetables in the summer. We _____ _____ buy any vegetables at the market.

◇ PRACTICE 18. Expressing necessity, lack of necessity, and prohibition. (Charts 7-9 and 7-10)

Directions: Complete each sentence with a form of ***have to*** or ***must***. Use the negative if necessary to make a sensible sentence.

1. Smoking in this building is prohibited. You _____*must/have to*_____ extinguish your cigar.

2. Alan's company pays all of his travel expenses. Alan _____*doesn't have to*_____ pay for his own plane ticket to the business conference in Amman, Jordan.

3. Our company provides free advice on the use of our products. You _____ pay us for the advice.

4. Everyone here _____ leave immediately! The building is on fire!

5. Lynn _____ attend the meeting tonight because she isn't working on the project that we're going to discuss. We're going to talk about raising money for the new library. Lynn isn't involved in that.

6. The construction company _____ finish the building by the end of the month. That's the date they promised, and they will lose a lot of money if they're late.

7. Please remember, you _____ call my house between three and four this afternoon. That's when the baby sleeps, and my mother will get upset if we wake him up.

◇ PRACTICE 19. Expressing necessity, lack of necessity, and prohibition. (Charts 7-9 and 7-10)

Directions: Write the phrases in the correct columns.

✓ *fall asleep while driving*	*take other people's belongings*
cook every meal themselves	*pay taxes*
say "sir" or "madam" to others	*stay in their homes in the evening*
eat and drink in order to live	*stop when they see a police car's lights*
drive without a license	*behind them*

People have to/must . . . (necessary)	People must not . . . (DON'T!)	People don't have to . . . (not necessary)
	fall asleep while driving	

◇ PRACTICE 20. Logical conclusion or necessity. (Charts 7-9 and 7-11)

Directions: Write **1** if the modal ***must*** expresses a logical conclusion. Write **2** if the modal expresses necessity.

1 = **logical conclusion.**
2 = **necessity.**

1. ___2___ You *must have* a passport to travel abroad.

2. ___1___ You *must like* to read. You have such a large library.

3. _____ Ellen *must like* fish. She buys it several times a week.

4. _____ You *must take off* your shoes before entering this room.

5. _____ The dessert *must be* good. It's almost gone.

6. _____ You *must try* this dessert. It's wonderful.

7. _____ Children *must stay* seated during the flight.

8. _____ You *must pay* in advance if you want a guaranteed seat for the performance.

9. _____ The cat *must be* afraid. She's hiding in the flower garden again.

◇ PRACTICE 21. Imperative sentences. (Chart 7-12)

Directions: Pretend that someone says the following sentences to **you**. Which verbs give **you** instructions? <u>Underline</u> the imperative verbs.

1. I'll be right back. <u>Wait</u> here.

2. <u>Don't wait</u> for Rebecca. She's not going to come.

3. Read pages thirty-nine to fifty-five before class tomorrow.

4. What are you doing? Don't put those magazines in the trash. I haven't read them yet.

5. Come in and have a seat. I'll be right with you.

6.

DON'T CROSS THIS FIELD UNLESS YOU CAN DO IT IN 9.9 SECONDS. THE BULL CAN DO IT IN 10. (NO TRESPASSING)

7. Don't just stand there! Do something!

8. A: Call me around eight, okay?

    B: Okay.

9. Here, little Mike. Take this apple to Daddy. That's good. Go ahead. Walk toward Daddy. That's great! Now give him the apple. Wonderful!

10. Capitalize the first word of each sentence. Put a period at the end of a sentence. If the sentence is a question, use a question mark at the end.

◇ **PRACTICE 22. Polite questions and imperatives.   (Charts 7-5, 7-6, and 7-12)**
Directions: Number the sentences in order of politeness.   **1 = most polite.**

1. __1__ Could you open the door?

    __3__ Open the door.

    __2__ Can you open the door?

2. ____ Get the phone, please.

    ____ Would you please get the phone?

    ____ Get the phone.

    ____ Can you get the phone?

3. ____ Can I borrow your eraser?

    ____ Could I borrow your eraser?

4. ____ Hand me the calculator.

    ____ Will you hand me the calculator, please?

    ____ Would you hand me the calculator, please?

    ____ Please hand me the calculator.

◇ **PRACTICE 23. LET'S and WHY DON'T.   (Chart 7-13)**
Directions: Complete the sentences with verbs from the list. The verbs may be used more than once.

ask	fly	pick up	see
call	get	play	stop
fill up	go	save	take

1. A: There's a strong wind today. Let's _____go_____ to the top of the hill on Cascade Avenue and _____fly_____ our kite.

    B: Sounds like fun. Why don't we _____see_____ if Louie wants to come with us?

    A: Okay. I'll call him.

2. A: What should we buy Mom for her birthday?

    B: I don't know. Let's _____ her some perfume or something.

    A: I have a better idea. Why don't we _____ her out for dinner and a movie?

3. A: My toe hurts. Let's not _____ dancing tonight.

    B: Okay. Why don't we _____ chess instead?

4. A: Let's _____ a taxi from the airport to the hotel.

   B: Why don't we _____ a bus and _____ ourselves some money?

5. A: We're almost out of gas. Why don't we _____ at a gas station and _____ before we drive the rest of the way to the beach?

   B: Okay. Are you hungry? I am. Let's _____ something to eat too.

   A: Great.

6. A: Let's _____ to a movie at the mall tonight.

   B: I've already seen all the good movies there. What else can we do?

   A: Well, Marika has a car. Why don't we _____ her and _____ if she wants to drive us into the city?

   B: Okay. What's her number?

◇ PRACTICE 24. Stating preferences. (Chart 7-14)
Directions: Complete the sentences with *prefer*, *like*, or *would rather*.

1. I _____prefer_____ cold weather to hot weather.

2. A: What's your favorite fruit?

   B: I _____like_____ strawberries better than any other fruit.

3. Mary _____would rather_____ save money than enjoy herself.

4. Unfortunately, many children _____ candy to vegetables.

5. A: Why isn't your brother going with us to the movie?

   B: He _____ stay home and read than go out on a Saturday night.

6. A: Does Peter _____ football to baseball?

   B: No. I think he _____ baseball better than football.

   A: Then why didn't he go to the game yesterday?

   B: Because he _____ watch sports on TV than go to a ball park.

7. I _____ jog in the morning than after work.

8. Heidi enjoys her independence. She is struggling to start her own business, but she _____ borrow money from the bank than ask her parents for help.

9. A: Do you want to go out to the Japanese restaurant for dinner?

   B: That would be okay, but in truth I _____ Chinese food to Japanese food.

   A: Really? I _____ Japanese food better than Chinese food. What shall we do?

   B: Let's go to the Italian restaurant.

10. A: Mother, I can't believe you have another cat! Now you have four cats, two dogs, and three birds.

    B: I know, dear. I can't help it. I love having animals around.

    A: Honestly, Mother, I sometimes think you _____ animals to people.

    B: Honestly, dear, sometimes I do.

◇ PRACTICE 25. Stating preferences. (Chart 7-14)
Directions: Use the words in parentheses to create a new sentence with the same meaning.

Example: Alex would rather swim than jog. *(prefer)*
   → *Alex prefers swimming to jogging.*

Example: My son likes fish better than beef. *(would rather)*
   → *My son would rather eat/have fish than beef.*

1. Kim likes salad better than dessert. *(prefer)*

2. In general, Nicole would rather have coffee than tea. *(like)*

3. Bill prefers teaching history to working as a business executive. *(would rather)*

4. When considering a pet, Sam prefers dogs to cats. *(like)*

5. On a long trip, Susie would rather drive than ride in the back seat. *(prefer)*

6. I like studying in a noisy room better than studying in a completely quiet room. *(would rather)*

7. Alex likes soccer better than baseball. *(would rather)*

◇ PRACTICE 26. Cumulative review. (Chapter 7)
Directions: Choose the best completion.

1. "I need the milk. _____ you get it out of the refrigerator for me?"
   "Sure."
   A. May   B. Should   C. Could

2. "_____ you hand me that book, please? I can't reach it."
   "Sure. Here it is."
   A. Would   B. Should   C. Must

3. "What do you like the most about your promotion?"
   "I _____ get up at 5:30 in the morning anymore. I can sleep until 7:00."
   A. must not   B. would rather   C. don't have to

4. "Do you have a minute? I need to talk to you."
   "I _____ leave here in ten minutes. Can we make an appointment for another time?"
   A. have to   B. could   C. may

5. "Yes? _____ I help you?"
   "Yes. Do you have these sandals in a size eight?"
   A. Should   B. Can   C. Will

6. "Let's go bowling Saturday afternoon."
   "Bowling? I _____ play golf than go bowling."
   A. had better   B. should   C. would rather

7. "Diane found a library book on a bench at Central Park. Someone had left it there."
   "She _____ take it to any library in the city. I'm sure they'll be glad to have it back."
   A. will   B. should   C. would rather

8. "Beth got another speeding ticket yesterday."
   "Oh? That's not good. She _____ be more careful. She'll end up in serious trouble if she gets any more."
   A. would rather   B. will   C. ought to

9. "Are you going to take the job transfer when the company moves out of town?"
   "I _____ accept their offer if they are willing to pay all of my moving expenses."
   A. must not   B. might   C. maybe

10. "Are you going to admit your mistake to the boss?"
    "Yes. I _____ tell her about it than have her hear about it from someone else."
    A. can   B. should   C. would rather

11. "I just heard that there's an accident on the freeway. Traffic is a mess."
    "We _____ leave earlier than we planned."
    A. maybe   B. had better   C. prefer to

12. "Would you like to go with me to the Williams' wedding next month?"
    "I'm not sure. I _____ be too busy with school."
    A. will   B. might   C. maybe

13. "Do you need help washing the dishes?"
    "Oh, no. You _____ help. There are enough people in the kitchen already."
        A. don't have to   B. must not   C. may not

14. "Why are you working so many evenings and weekends?"
    "I _____ increase sales or I'm in danger of losing my job."
        A. may   B. can   C. have got to

15. "Are these gloves necessary?"
    "Yes. You _____ use this chemical without gloves. It will burn your skin."
        A. must not   B. don't have to   C. could not

◇ PRACTICE 27. Cumulative review. (Chapter 7)
   Directions: Correct the errors.

                                    had to
 1. Before I left on my trip last month, I ~~must~~ get a passport.

 2. Could you to bring us more coffee, please?

 3. Ben can driving, but he prefers take the bus.

 4. My roommate maybe at home this evening.

 5. A few of our classmates can't to come to the school picnic.

 6. May you take our picture, please?

 7. Jane's eyes are red, and she is yawning. She must is sleepy.

 8. Jim would rather has Fridays off in the summer than a long vacation.

 9. I must reading several lengthy books for my literature class.

10. Take your warm clothes with you. It will maybe snow.

11. When the baby went to the doctor last week, she must has several shots.

12. It's very cool in here. Please you turn up the heat.

13. You had better to call us before you come over. We're often away during the day.

14. The children would rather to see the circus than a baseball game.

15. It's such a gorgeous day. Why we don't go to a park or the beach?

◇ **PRACTICE 28. Cumulative review. (Chapter 7)**

Directions: The topic of this passage is writing a composition. Read the passage through completely to get the main ideas. Then read it again slowly and choose from the words in ***boldface italics***.

Writing a Composition

(1) "What? Not another composition! I hate writing compositions. I'm not good at it." Do you ever complain about having to write compositions in English class? A lot of students do. You **(may,)** ***cannot*** find it difficult and time-consuming, but you are learning a useful skill. The ability to write clearly ***is, must be*** important. It ***can, must*** affect your success in school and in your job. You ***may, can*** learn to write effectively by practicing. One of the best ways to practice your writing skills is to prepare compositions in a thoughtful, step-by-step process.

(2) The first step in writing a composition is to choose a subject that interests you. You ***maybe, should*** write about a subject you already know about or ***can, have to*** find out about through research. Writers ***might, should*** never pretend to be experts. For example, if you have never bought a car and are not knowledgeable about automobiles, you ***should, should not*** write an essay on what to look for when buying a car—unless, of course, you plan to research the subject in books and magazines and make yourself an expert. There is one topic about which you are the most knowledgeable expert in the world, and that topic ***is, may be*** yourself and your experiences. Many of the most interesting and informative compositions are based simply on a writer's personal experience and observations. The questions you should ask yourself when choosing a topic are "Do I have any expertise in this subject?" and if not, "***Will, Can*** I be able to find information about this subject?"

(3) After you have a topic and have researched it if necessary, start writing down your thoughts. These notes ***must not, do not have to*** be in any particular order. You ***do not have to, could not*** worry about grammar at this time. You ***can, may*** pay special attention to that later.

(4) Next, you ***have to, may*** organize your thoughts. You ***cannot, might not*** say everything possible about a subject in one composition. Therefore, you ***may, must*** carefully choose the ideas and information you want to include. Look over your notes, think hard about your topic, and find a central idea. Answer these questions: "What ***am, do*** I want my readers to understand? What ***is, does*** my main idea? How ***can, am*** I put this idea into one sentence?" Good writing depends on clear thinking. Writers ***should, had better*** spend more time thinking than actually writing. After you have a clearly formed main idea, choose relevant information from your notes to include in your composition.

(5) Before you begin to write the actual composition, you **ought to, can** know exactly what you want to say and how you are going to develop your ideas. Many good writers **prepare, prepared** an outline before they start. An outline is like a road map to keep you headed toward your destination without getting lost or sidetracked.

(6) There **are, ought to be** many ways to begin a composition. For example, you **might, must** begin with a story that leads up to your main idea. Or you **may, ought to** start with a question that you want your reader to think about, and then suggest an answer. **Maybe, May be** you **could, have to** introduce your topic by defining a key word. Simply presenting factual information **is, will be** another common way of beginning a composition. Your goals in your first paragraph **is, are** to catch your reader's attention and then state your main idea clearly and concisely. By the end of the first paragraph, your reader **may, should** understand what you are going to cover in the composition.

(7) If possible, write the entire first draft of your composition in a single sitting. After you have a first draft, the next step is rewriting. Every composition **could, should** go through several drafts. Rewriting is a natural part of the process of writing. You **will, do not have to** find many things that you **can change, changed** and improve when you reread your first draft. As you revise, you **will, should** be careful to include connecting words such as *then, next, for example, after,* and *therefore.* These words connect one idea to another so that your reader will not get lost. Also pay attention to grammar, punctuation, and spelling as you revise and rewrite. Your dictionary **should, can** be next to you, or if you are working on a computer, you **should, must** use the "spell checker."

(8) Writing **is, may be** a skill. It improves as you gain experience with the process of choosing a subject, jotting down thoughts, organizing them into a first draft, and then rewriting and polishing. At the end of this process, you **should, must** have a clear and well-written composition.

Index

# Answer Key

To the student: To make it easy to correct your answers, remove this answer key along the perforations and make a separate answer key booklet for yourself.

Chapter 1: PRESENT TIME

◇ **PRACTICE 1, p. 1.**

A: Hi. My name ____**is**____ Kunio.
B: Hi. My ____**name is**____ Maria. I ___**'m**___ glad to meet you.
KUNIO: I ____**am**____ glad to ____**meet**____ you, too. Where ____**are you from**____?
MARIA: I ____**am**____ from Mexico. Where ____**are you from**____?
KUNIO: I ____**am from**____ Japan.
MARIA: Where ____**are you**____ living now?
KUNIO: On Fifth Avenue in an apartment. And you?
MARIA: I ____**am**____ living in a dorm.
KUNIO: What ____**are**____ you studying?
MARIA: Business. After I study English, I am going to attend the School of Business Administration. How ____**about**____ you? What ____**is**____ your major?
KUNIO: Engineering.
MARIA: What ____**do**____ you like to do in your free time?
KUNIO: I read a lot. How ____**about**____ you?
MARIA: I like to get on the Internet.
KUNIO: Really? What ____**do**____ you do when you're online?
MARIA: I visit many different Web sites. It ____**is**____ a good way to practice my English.
KUNIO: That's interesting. I ____**like**____ to get on the Internet, too.
MARIA: I have to ____**write**____ your full name on the board when I introduce you to the class. How ____**do you**____ spell your name?
KUNIO: My first name ____**is**____ Kunio. K-U-N-I-O. My family name ____**is**____ Akiwa.
MARIA: Kunio Akiwa. ____**Is**____ that right?
KUNIO: Yes, it ____**is**____. And what ____**is**____ your name again?
MARIA: My first name ____**is**____ Maria. M-A-R-I-A. My last name ____**is**____ Lopez.
KUNIO: Thanks. It's been nice talking to you.
MARIA: I enjoyed it, too.

◇ **PRACTICE 2, p. 2.**

1. am sitting
2. am reading
3. am looking
4. am writing
5. am doing
6. sit . . . am sitting
7. read . . . am reading
8. look . . . am looking
9. write . . . am writing
10. do . . . am doing

◇ **PRACTICE 3, p. 2.**

PART I.
1. speak
2. speak
3. speaks
4. speak
5. speaks

PART III.
11. Do you speak
12. Do they speak
13. Does he speak
14. Do we speak
15. Does she speak

PART II.
6. do not (don't) speak
7. do not (don't) speak
8. does not (doesn't) speak
9. do not (don't) speak
10. does not (doesn't) speak

◇ **PRACTICE 4, p. 3.**

PART I.
1. am speaking
2. are speaking
3. is speaking
4. are speaking
5. is speaking

PART III.
11. Are you speaking
12. Is he speaking
13. Are they speaking
14. Are we speaking
15. Is she speaking

PART II.
6. am not speaking
7. are not speaking
8. is not speaking
9. are not speaking
10. is not speaking

◇ **PRACTICE 5, p. 3.**

1. Is he
2. Does he
3. Does he
4. Is he
5. Does he
6. Is he
7. Is he
8. Does he
9. Does he
10. Is he

◇ PRACTICE 6, p. 4.

1. Is she	6. Does she
2. Does she	7. Is she
3. Is she	8. Is she
4. Is she	9. Does she
5. Does she	10. Is she

◇ PRACTICE 7, p. 4.

1. does	7. do
2. Do	8. Ø . . . Ø
3. Ø	9. does
4. Does	10. Ø
5. Ø	11. Do
6. Ø	

◇ PRACTICE 8, p. 5.

1. is	7. Ø	13. am
2. are	8. is	14. are
3. is	9. Are	15. Ø
4. Is	10. Do	16. am
5. does	11. Ø	17. Do
6. Ø	12. are	

◇ PRACTICE 9, p. 5.

1. Ø	5. Are	9. Ø
2. Do	6. are	10. is
3. Does	7. Ø	11. Do
4. Is	8. are	

◇ PRACTICE 10, p. 6.

1. is	7. Ø	13. is
2. are	8. do	14. Ø . . . Ø
3. Ø	9. Ø	15. is
4. Does	10. does	16. Ø . . . are
5. do	11. does	17. Do
6. Ø	12. Ø	18. Does

◇ PRACTICE 11, p. 7.

1. usually . . . Ø	7. sometimes . . . Ø
2. Ø . . . usually	8. never . . . Ø
3. always . . . Ø	9. Ø . . . never
4. Ø . . . always	10. Ø . . . usually . . . Ø
5. usually . . . Ø	11. Ø . . . always . . . Ø
6. Ø . . . always	12. Ø . . . always

◇ PRACTICE 12, p. 7.

1. a. usually doesn't come	2. a. usually isn't
b. doesn't ever come	b. is rarely
c. seldom comes	c. isn't always
d. sometimes comes	d. frequently isn't
e. always comes	e. is never
f. occasionally comes	f. isn't ever
g. never comes	g. is seldom
h. hardly ever comes	

◇ PRACTICE 13, p. 8.

1. always wakes	5. seldom surfs
2. sometimes skips	6. usually talks
3. frequently visits	7. rarely does
4. is usually	8. is never

◇ PRACTICE 14, p. 8.

1. often OR usually	7. seldom OR rarely
2. seldom OR rarely	8. seldom OR rarely
3. always	9. never
4. often OR usually	10. always
5. sometimes	11. often OR usually
6. usually	12. seldom

◇ PRACTICE 15, p. 9.

1. always chooses	7. often OR usually gets
2. seldom OR rarely go	8. sometimes gets
3. sometimes ride	9. seldom OR rarely finishes
4. seldom OR rarely exercises	10. never play
5. never eat	11. usually arrives
6. is always	12. always take

◇ PRACTICE 16, p. 10.

1. like**s**	11. Ø
2. watch**es**	12. Do**es** . . . Ø
3. do**es**n't . . . Ø	13. do**es**n't
4. Ø	14. carr**ies**
5. Ø . . . Ø	15. play**s**
6. Do**es** . . . Ø	16. live**s**
7. like**s**	17. Ø
8. wash**es**	18. visit**s**
9. go**es**	19. catch**es**
10. get**s**	20. Ø

◇ PRACTICE 17, p. 11.

Sam **leaves** his apartment at 8:00 every morning. **He walks** to the bus stop and **catches** the 8:10 bus. It takes him downtown. Then he **transfers** to another bus, and it takes him to his part-time job. **He arrives** at work at 8:50. **He stays** until 1:00, and then **he leaves** for school. **He attends** classes until 5:00. **He** usually **studies** in the library and **tries** to finish his homework. Then **he goes** home around 8:00. **He has** a long day.

◇ PRACTICE 18, p. 11.

/s/	/z/	/əz/
cooks	stays	promises
invites	seems	watches
hates	travels	misses
picks	draws	introduces

◇ PRACTICE 19, p. 12.

1. /z/	6. /z/	11. /əz/
2. /s/	7. /əz/	12. /z/
3. /əz/	8. /s/	13. /s/
4. /z/	9. /z/	14. /z/
5. /z/	10. /əz/	15. /s/

◇ PRACTICE 20, p. 12.

	simple pres.	*pres. prog.*
1.	buys	is buying
2.	comes	is coming
3.	opens	is opening
4.	begins	is beginning
5.	stops	is stopping
6.	dies	is dying

simple pres.	pres. prog.
7. rains	is raining
8. dreams	is dreaming
9. eats	is eating
10. enjoys	is enjoying
11. writes	is writing
12. tries	is trying
13. stays	is staying
14. hopes	is hoping
15. studies	is studying
16. lies	is lying
17. flies	is flying
18. sits	is sitting

◇ PRACTICE 21, p. 12.

1. a	5. a	9. b
2. a	6. a	10. b
3. a	7. b	11. b
4. b	8. a	12. a

◇ PRACTICE 22, p. 13.

1. is snowing	8. is looking . . . sees
2. takes	9. sings
3. drive	10. bite
4. am watching	11. writes
5. prefer	12. understand
6. need	13. belongs
7. are playing	14. is shining . . . is raining

◇ PRACTICE 23, p. 14.

1. usually doesn't take	9. is hugging
2. needs	10. are playing
3. is enjoying	11. is waving
4. are	12. is walking
5. are eating	13. (is) entertaining
6. are drinking	14. is smiling
7. (are) reading	15. usually takes
8. is working	16. is

◇ PRACTICE 24, p. 15.

1. My friend **doesn't** speak English well.
2. I **don't** believe you.
3. My sister's dog **doesn't** bark.
4. Our teacher **always starts** class on time.
5. Look! The cat **is getting** up on the counter.
6. **Does** Marie **have** enough money?
7. We **don't like** this rainy weather.
8. Mrs. Gray is **worrying** about her daughter. OR
   Mrs. Gray **worries** about her daughter.
9. My brother **doesn't have** enough free time.
10. **Does** Jim drive to school every day?
11. He always **hurries** in the morning. He **doesn't want** to be late.
12. Anna **usually has** dinner at eight.

◇ PRACTICE 25, p. 15.

1. A: Are
   B: I am OR I'm not
2. A: Do
   B: they do OR they don't
3. A: Do
   B: I do OR I don't

4. A: Does
   B: she does OR she doesn't
5. A: Are
   B: they are OR they aren't
6. A: Do
   B: they do OR they don't
7. A: Is
   B: he is OR he isn't
8. A: Are
   B: I am OR I'm not
9. A: Is
   B: it is OR it isn't
10. A: Do
    B: we do OR we don't

◇ PRACTICE 26, p. 16.

1. A: are you doing
   B: am watching . . . want
   A: enjoy . . . go . . . is . . . run
   B: are making
2. A: Do you read
   B: do . . . read . . . subscribe . . . always look
3. am I studying . . . do I want . . . need
4. A: am leaving . . . Do you want
   B: am waiting
5. B: Is the baby sleeping
   A: is taking
   B: don't want
6. goes . . . likes . . . is preparing
7. is . . . is blowing . . . are falling
8. eats . . . don't eat . . . do you eat
9. A: Do you shop
   B: don't . . . usually shop
   A: are you shopping
   B: am trying
10. lose . . . rest . . . grow . . . keep . . . stay . . . don't grow . . . don't have . . . is . . . grow

Chapter 2: PAST TIME

◇ PRACTICE 1, p. 18.

1. walked . . . yesterday
2. talked . . . last
3. opened . . . yesterday
4. went . . . last
5. met . . . last
6. Yesterday . . . made . . . took
7. paid . . . last
8. Yesterday . . . fell
9. left . . . last

◇ PRACTICE 2, p. 19.

1. started	11. fell	21. took
2. went	12. heard	22. paid
3. saw	13. sang	23. left
4. stood	14. explored	24. wore
5. arrived	15. asked	25. opened
6. won	16. brought	26. decided
7. had	17. broke	27. planned
8. made	18. ate	28. wrote
9. finished	19. watched	29. taught
10. felt	20. built	30. held

◇ PRACTICE 3, p. 19.

1. A: Did you answer
   B: I did. I answered OR I didn't. I didn't answer
2. A: Did he see
   B: he did. He saw OR he didn't. He didn't see
3. A: Did they watch
   B: they did. They watched OR they didn't. They
   didn't watch
4. A: Did you understand
   B: I did. I understood OR I didn't. I didn't
   understand
5. A: Were you
   B: I was. I was OR I wasn't. I wasn't

◇ PRACTICE 4, p. 20.

1. didn't fly . . . walked/took the bus
2. aren't . . . are sour
3. didn't walk . . . walked on the moon
4. wasn't a baby . . . was *(number of years old)*
5. didn't come . . . came
6. doesn't come . . . comes from coffee beans
7. didn't sleep . . . slept inside
8. isn't . . . is cold
9. didn't disappear . . . disappeared millions of years

◇ PRACTICE 5, p. 21.

1. Did he study	5. Were they hungry
2. Was he sick	6. Did you go
3. Was she sad	7. Did she understand
4. Did they eat	8. Did he forget

◇ PRACTICE 6, p. 21.

1. Did	5. Was
2. Were	6. Did
3. Did	7. Was
4. Did	8. Did

◇ PRACTICE 7, p. 22.

1. shook	5. held	9. thought
2. stayed	6. fought	10. called
3. swam	7. taught	11. rode
4. jumped	8. froze	12. sold

◇ PRACTICE 9, p. 23.

1. /t/	8. /t/	15. /t/
2. /d/	9. /d/	16. /d/
3. /əd/	10. /əd/	17. /t/
4. /d/	11. /d/	18. /əd/
5. /əd/	12. /t/	19. /d/
6. /əd/	13. /t/	20. /t/
7. /d/	14. /əd/	

◇ PRACTICE 10, p. 23.

	spelling	pron.
1.	walk**ed**	/t/
2.	pat**ted**	/əd/
3.	wor**ried**	/d/
4.	stay**ed**	/d/
5.	visit**ed**	/əd/
6.	die**d**	/d/
7.	trade**d**	/əd/
8.	plan**ned**	/d/
9.	open**ed**	/d/

10.	hur**ried**	/d/
11.	rent**ed**	/əd/
12.	tr**ied**	/d/
13.	enjoy**ed**	/d/
14.	stop**ped**	/t/
15.	need**ed**	/əd/

◇ PRACTICE 12 p. 24.

double consonant?	-ING	-ED
no	exciting	excited
no	existing	existed
no	shouting	shouted
yes	patting	patted
no	visiting	visited
yes	admitting	admitted
no	praying	prayed
no	prying	pried
no	tying	tied

◇ PRACTICE 13, p. 25.

double

consonant	drop -E	add -ING
hitting	coming	learning
cutting	taking	listening
hopping	hoping	raining
beginning	smiling	staying
winning	writing	studying

◇ PRACTICE 14, p. 25.

	-ING	-ED
1.	riding	(ridden)
2.	starting	started
3.	coming	(came)
4.	happening	happened
5.	trying	tried
6.	buying	(bought)
7.	hoping	hoped
8.	keeping	(kept)
9.	tipping	tipped
10.	failing	failed
11.	filling	filled
12.	feeling	(felt)
13.	dining	dined
14.	meaning	(meant)
15.	winning	(won)
16.	learning	learned
17.	listening	listened
18.	beginning	(began)

◇ PRACTICE 15, p. 26.

	-ing	simple form
1.	waiting	wait
2.	petting	pet
3.	biting	bite
4.	sitting	sit
5.	writing	write
6.	fighting	fight
7.	waiting	wait
8.	getting	get
9.	starting	start
10.	permitting	permit
11.	lifting	lift
12.	eating	eat

-ing	simple form
13. tasting	taste
14. cutting	cut
15. meeting	meet
16. visiting	visit

◇ PRACTICE 16, p. 27.

PART I.	PART IV.
bought	**broke**
brought	**wrote**
taught	**froze**
caught	**rode**
fought	**sold**
thought	**stole**
found	
	PART V.
PART II.	hit
sw**am**	hurt
dr**ank**	read
s**ang**	shut
r**ang**	cost
	put
PART III.	quit
blew	
drew	PART VI.
flew	paid
grew	said
kn**ew**	
threw	

◇ PRACTICE 17, p. 28.

1. drank/had		11. ran
2. ate		12. led
3. began . . . shut		13. paid
4. rang		14. froze
5. came		15. did
6. built		16. rose
7. fell . . . hurt		17. thought
8. stole/took		18. wrote
9. shut		19. kept
10. drove		20. built

◇ PRACTICE 18, p. 29.

1. spoke	11. gave . . . spoke
2. dug	12. grew
3. chose	13. forgot
4. lost	14. bought/read
5. quit	15. shook
6. slept	16. stole
7. found	17. felt
8. cut	18. drew
9. met	19. heard
10. taught	20. fell . . . broke

◇ PRACTICE 19, p. 30.

	question	negative
1.	Did I ride	I didn't ride
2.	Did she sit	She didn't sit
3.	Were we	We weren't
4.	Did they try	They didn't try
5.	Was he	He wasn't
6.	Did they cut	They didn't cut
7.	Did she throw	She didn't throw
8.	Did we do	We didn't do

◇ PRACTICE 20, p. 31.

1. What did you do last night?
2. What is your friend's name?
3. Is he nice?
4. How was your evening?
5. Where did you go?
6. Did you enjoy it?
7. Was the music loud?
8. What time did you get home?
9. What did you wear?
10. What is he like?
11. What does he look like?
12. Do you want to go out with him again?

◇ PRACTICE 21, p. 32.

	every day	now	yesterday
1.	is	is	was
2.	think	**am thinking**	thought
3.	play	**are playing**	**played**
4.	**drink**	**am drinking**	drank
5.	**teaches**	is teaching	**taught**
6.	**swims**	**is swimming**	swam
7.	sleep	**are sleeping**	**slept**
8.	**reads**	is reading	**read**
9.	**try**	**are trying**	tried
10.	eat	**are eating**	**ate**

◇ PRACTICE 22, p. 32.

1. A: Did you hear
   B: didn't . . . didn't hear . . . was
2. A: Do you hear
   B: don't . . . don't hear
3. A: Did you build
   B: didn't . . . built
4. A: Is a fish
   B: it is
   A: Are they
   B: they are . . . don't know
5. A: want . . . Do you want
   B: have . . . bought . . . don't need
6. offer . . . is . . . offered . . . didn't accept
7. took . . . found . . . didn't know . . . isn't . . . didn't want
   . . . went . . . made . . . heated . . . seemed . . . am not
8. likes . . . worry . . . is . . . trust . . . graduated . . . went
   . . . didn't travel . . . rented . . . rode . . . was . . . worried
   . . . were . . . saw . . . knew

◇ PRACTICE 23, p. 34.

1. were hiding
2. were singing
3. was watching
4. were talking
5. were reading . . . were sitting . . . (were) looking

◇ PRACTICE 24, p. 34.

1. was playing . . . broke		6. picked up . . . was hiking
2. scored . . . was playing		7. tripped . . . fell . . .
3. hurt . . . was playing		was dancing
4. was hiking . . . found		8. was dancing . . . met
5. saw . . . was hiking		9. was dancing . . . got

◇ **PRACTICE 25, p. 35.**
1. began . . . were walking
2. was washing . . . dropped . . . broke
3. saw . . . was eating . . . (was) talking . . . joined
4. was walking . . . fell . . . hit
5. was singing . . . didn't hear
6. was walking . . . heard . . . was
7. A: Did your lights go out
   B: was . . . was taking . . . found . . . ate . . . tried . . . went . . . slept
8. went . . . saw . . . had . . . were walking . . . began . . . dried . . . were passing . . . lowered . . . started . . . stretched . . . tried . . . didn't let . . . was standing . . . pointed . . . said

◇ **PRACTICE 26, p. 36.**
1. I gave Alan his allowance <u>after he finished his chores.</u>
   OR
   <u>After Alan finished his chores,</u> I gave him his allowance.
2. The doorbell rang <u>while I was climbing the stairs.</u> OR
   <u>While I was climbing the stairs,</u> the doorbell rang.
3. The firefighters checked the ashes one last time <u>before they went home.</u> OR
   <u>Before they went home,</u> the firefighters checked the ashes one last time.
4. <u>When the Novaks stopped by our table at the restaurant,</u> they showed us their new baby. OR
   The Novaks showed us their new baby <u>when they stopped by our table at the restaurant.</u>
5. We started to dance <u>as soon as the music began.</u> OR
   <u>As soon as the music began,</u> we started to dance.
6. We stayed in our seats <u>until the game ended.</u> OR
   <u>Until the game ended,</u> we stayed in our seats.
7. <u>While my father was listening to a baseball game on the radio,</u> he was watching a basketball game on television.
   OR
   My father was watching a basketball game on television <u>while he was listening to a baseball game on the radio.</u>

◇ **PRACTICE 27, p. 37.**
1. was
2. slept
3. came
4. packed
5. took
6. spent
7. got
8. found
9. fed
10. threw
11. swam
12. caught
13. hit
14. stole
15. were feeding
16. met
17. comes
18. sat
19. spoke
20. ate
21. took
22. was sleeping
23. bit
24. woke
25. heard
26. looked
27. saw
28. flew
29. did
30. took
31. got
32. read
33. is
34. drew
35. played
36. won
37. won
38. taught
39. were playing
40. fell
41. found
42. joined
43. were
44. were
45. hurt
46. was
47. left
48. was

◇ **PRACTICE 28, p. 39.**
1. used to hate school
2. used to be a secretary
3. used to have a rat
4. used to go bowling
5. used to have fresh eggs
6. used to crawl under his bed . . . put his hands over his ears
7. used to go
8. didn't use/used to wear
9. used to hate . . . didn't use/used to have
10. did you use/used to do

◇ **PRACTICE 29, p. 40.**
1. They **didn't stay** at the park very long last Saturday
2. They ~~are~~ walked to school yesterday.
3. I ~~was~~ **understood** all the teacher's questions yesterday.
4. We didn't **know** what to do when the fire alarm **rang** yesterday.
5. I ~~was~~ really enjoyed the baseball game last week.
6. Mr. Rice didn't **die** in the accident.
7. I **used** to live with my parents, but now I have my own apartment.
8. My friends ~~were~~ went on vacation together last month.
9. I **wasn't** afraid of anything when I **was** a child.
10. The teacher ~~was~~ changed his mind yesterday.
11. Sally **loved** Jim, but he didn't **love** her.
12. Carmen **didn't use/used** to eat fish, but now she does.

◇ **PRACTICE 30, p. 41.**
1. was preparing
2. rang
3. put
4. rushed
5. opened
6. found
7. was holding
8. needed
9. was dealing
10. rang
11. excused
12. reached
13. was trying
14. ran
15. was trying
16. were swimming
17. said
18. hung
19. thanked
20. shut
21. yelled
22. shooed
23. sat
24. stayed
25. began
26. felt
27. rang
28. rang

Chapter 3: FUTURE TIME

◇ **PRACTICE 1, p. 43.**
1. a. arrives
   b. arrived
   c. is going to arrive OR will arrive
2. a. eats
   b. ate
   c. is going to eat OR will eat
3. a. doesn't arrive
   b. didn't arrive
   c. isn't going to arrive OR will not/won't arrive
4. a. Do . . . eat
   b. Did . . . eat
   c. Are . . . going to eat OR Will . . . eat
5. a. don't eat
   b. didn't eat
   c. 'm/am not going to eat OR will not/won't eat

◇ **PRACTICE 2, p. 44.**

be going to	*will*
am going to	will
are going to	will
is going to	will
are going to	will
are going to	will
are not going to	will not
is not going to	will not
am not going to	will not

◇ PRACTICE 3, p. 44.

1. I'm going to eat
2. he isn't going to be
3. they're going to take
4. she's going to walk
5. it isn't going to rain
6. we're going to be
7. you aren't going to hitchhike
8. I'm not going to get
9. he isn't going to wear

◇ PRACTICE 4, p. 44.

The Smiths **will** celebrate their 50th wedding anniversary on December 1 of this year. Their children are planning a party for them at a local hotel. Their family and friends **will** join them for the celebration.

Mr. and Mrs. Smith have three children and five grandchildren. The Smiths know that two of their children **will** be at the party, but the third child, their youngest daughter, is far away in Africa, where she is doing medical research. They believe she **will** not come home for the party.

The Smiths don't know it, but their youngest daughter **will** be at the party. She is planning to surprise them. It **will** be a wonderful surprise for them! They **will** be very happy to see her. The whole family **will** enjoy being together for this special occasion.

◇ PRACTICE 5, p. 45.

1. Will Nick start
   Is Nick going to start
2. Will Mr. Jones give
   Is Mr. Jones going to give
3. Will Jacob quit
   Is Jacob going to quit
4. Will Mr. and Mrs. Kono adopt
   Are Mr. and Mrs. Kono going to adopt
5. Will the Johnsons move
   Are the Johnsons going to move
6. Will Dr. Johnson retire
   Is Dr. Johnson going to retire

◇ PRACTICE 6, p. 46.

1. A: Will you help
   B: I will OR I won't
2. A: Will Paul lend
   B: he will OR he won't
3. A: Will Jane graduate
   B: she will OR she won't
4. A: Will her parents be
   B: they will OR they won't
5. A: Will I benefit
   B: you will OR you won't

◇ PRACTICE 7, p. 46.

1. probably won't
2. will probably
3. will probably
4. probably won't
5. will probably
6. probably won't
7. will probably
8. will probably

◇ PRACTICE 8, p. 47.

PART I.
1. I'll probably go
2. she probably won't come
3. he will probably go
4. he probably won't hand
5. they will probably have

PART II.
6. I'm probably going to watch
7. I'm probably not going to be
8. it's probably going to be
9. they probably aren't going to come
10. she probably isn't going to ride

◇ PRACTICE 9, p. 47.

1. 90%   5. 50%
2. 50%   6. 90%
3. 100%   7. 100%
4. 90%   8. 50%

◇ PRACTICE 10, p. 48.

1. are probably going to have
2. are probably not going to invite
3. may get married . . . Maybe . . . will get married
4. may rent
5. will probably decide
6. may not be . . . may be
7. will go
8. probably won't go

◇ PRACTICE 11, p. 49.

1. 'll answer it   5. 'll turn . . . off
2. 'll hold   6. 'll leave
3. 'll take   7. 'll get
4. 'll move   8. 'll read

◇ PRACTICE 12, p. 49.

1. 'm going to
2. 'll
3. 'm going to
4. 'll
5. 'm going to
6. 'll
7. 'm going to . . . 'll

◇ PRACTICE 13, p. 50.

1. 'll   7. 'm going to
2. 'm going to   8. 'll
3. 'm going to   9. 's going to
4. 'm going to   10. 'll put
5. A: are . . . going to 11. 'm going to
   B: 'm going to   12. 'll
6. 'll

◇ PRACTICE 14, p. 52.

Time clauses:
1. After I did my homework last night
2. after I do my homework tonight
3. Before Bob left for work this morning
4. Before Bob leaves for work this morning
5. after I get home this evening

Time clauses:
6. after I got home last night
7. as soon as the teacher arrives
8. As soon as the teacher arrived
9. When the rain stops
10. when the rain stopped

◇ PRACTICE 15, p. 52.
1. After I finish . . . I'm going to go
2. I'm not going to go . . . until I finish
3. Before Ann watches . . . she will (she'll) finish
4. Jim is going to read . . . after he gets
5. When I call . . . I'll ask
6. Mrs. Fox will stay . . . until she finishes
7. As soon as I get . . . I'm going to take
8. While I am . . . I'm going to go

◇ PRACTICE 16, p. 53.
1. If it rains tomorrow,
2. If it's hot tomorrow,
3. if he has enough time
4. If I don't get a check tomorrow,
5. if the weather is nice tomorrow
6. If Gina doesn't study for her test,
7. if I have enough money
8. If I don't study tonight,

◇ PRACTICE 17, p. 54.
1. <u>When I see you Sunday afternoon,</u> I'll give you my answer OR
   I'll give you my answer <u>when I see you Sunday afternoon.</u>
2. <u>Before my friends come over,</u> I'm going to clean up my apartment. OR
   I'm going to clean up my apartment <u>before my friends come over.</u>
3. <u>When the storm is over,</u> I'm going to do some errands. OR
   I'm going to do some errands <u>when the storm is over.</u>
4. <u>If you don't learn how to use a computer,</u> you will have trouble finding a job. OR
   You will have trouble finding a job <u>if you don't learn how to use a computer.</u>
5. <u>As soon as Joe finishes his report,</u> he'll meet us at the coffee shop. OR
   Joe will meet us at the coffee shop <u>as soon as he finishes his report.</u>
6. <u>After Sue washes and dries the dishes,</u> she will put them away. OR
   Sue will put the dishes away <u>after she washes and dries them.</u>
7. <u>If they don't leave at seven,</u> they won't get to the theater on time. OR
   They won't get to the theater on time <u>if they don't leave at seven.</u>

◇ PRACTICE 18, p. 54.
PART II.
(1) Tomorrow morning **will be** an ordinary morning. I **'ll get** up at 6:30. I **'ll wash** my face and **brush** my teeth. Then I **'ll** probably put on my jeans and a sweater. I **'ll** go to the kitchen and **start** the electric coffee maker.

(2) Then I **'ll walk** down my driveway to get the morning newspaper. If I **see** a deer in my garden, I **'ll** watch it for a while and then **make** some noise to chase it away before it **destroys** my flowers.

(3) As soon as I **get** back to the kitchen, I'll **pour** myself a cup of coffee and **open** the morning paper. While I'm reading the paper, my teenage daughter **will come** downstairs. We **'ll talk** about her plans for the day. I **'ll help** her with her breakfast and **make** a lunch for her to take to school. After we **say** goodbye, I **'ll eat** some fruit and cereal and **finish** reading the paper.

(4) Then I **'ll go** to my office. My office **is** in my home. My office **has** a desk, a computer, a radio, a fax, a copy machine, and a lot of bookshelves. I **'ll work** all morning. While I'm working, the phone **will ring** many times. I **'ll talk** to many people. At 11:30, I **'ll go** to the kitchen and **make** a sandwich for lunch. As I said, it **will be** an ordinary morning.

◇ PRACTICE 19, p. 56.
1. I'm going to stay . . . I'm staying
2. They're going to travel . . . They're traveling
3. We're going to get . . . We're getting
4. He's going to start . . . He's starting
5. She's going to go . . . She's going
6. My neighbors are going to build . . . My neighbors are building

◇ PRACTICE 20, p. 56.
1. is traveling
2. are arriving
3. 'm/am meeting
4. 'm/am getting
5. is . . . taking
6. 'm/am studying
7. 'm/am leaving
8. is attending . . . 'm/am seeing
9. is speaking
10. are coming . . . 'm/am planning . . . 'm/am preparing
11. 'm/am calling

◇ PRACTICE 21, p. 58.
1. A: does . . . begin/start
   B: begins/starts
2. opens
3. arrives/gets in
4. begins
5. A: does . . . close
   B: closes
6. open . . . starts/begins . . . arrive . . . ends/finishes
7. A: does . . . depart/leave
   B: leaves
   A: does . . . arrive/land

◇ PRACTICE 22, p. 59.
1. is about to rain
2. is about to leave
3. is about to write
4. is about to ring
5. is . . . about to break

◇ PRACTICE 23, p. 59.

1. study	6. is writing . . . waiting
2. set	7. takes . . . buys
3. doing	8. go . . . tell
4. go	9. 'm/am taking . . . forgetting
5. fell	10. will discover . . . (will) apologize

◇ PRACTICE 24, p. 60.

1. My friends will ~~to~~ join us after work.
2. Maybe the rain **will stop / is going to stop** soon.
3. On Friday, our school **is closing / will close / is going to close** early so teachers can go to a workshop.
4. My husband and I ~~will~~ intend to be at your graduation.
5. Our company is going to **sell** computer equipment to schools.
6. Give grandpa a hug. He's about to **leave**.
7. Mr. Scott is going to retire and **move** to a warmer climate.
8. If your soccer team ~~will~~ **wins** the championship tomorrow, we'll have a big celebration for you.
9. **Maybe I** won't be able to meet you for coffee. OR
   I **may not** be able to meet you for coffee. OR
   I ~~maybe~~ won't be able to meet you for coffee.
10. I bought this cloth because I **am going to** make some curtains for my bedroom.
11. I **am** (I'm) **moving** / **will move** / **am going to move** to London when I ~~will~~ finish my education here.
12. Are you going **to** go to the meeting?
13. I opened the door and **walked** to the front of the room.
14. When will you ~~be going to~~ move into your new apartment? OR
    When **are** you going to move into your new apartment? OR
    When **are** you **moving** into your new apartment?

◇ PRACTICE 25, p. 61.

1. go . . . am going to finish / will finish . . . write
2. was making . . . spilled . . . caught . . . started . . . ran . . . thought
3. plays . . . cuts . . . is not doing . . . doesn't study . . . go . . . will flunk / is going to flunk
4. cries . . . stomps . . . gets . . . got . . . picked . . . threw . . . didn't hit . . . felt . . . apologized . . . kissed
5. is beginning . . . begins . . . don't like . . . think . . . are going to take / will take . . . is . . . are going to drive / will drive . . . enjoy
6. is going to meet / will meet . . . arrives
7. see . . . am going to tell / will tell
8. am . . . see
9. am . . . will stay
10. are going to go / will go . . . is
11. is watching . . . is . . . is going to mow / will mow
12. was . . . left
13. get . . . run
14. don't need
15. is planning / plans . . . Are you going to come / Are you coming
16. A: do you usually get
    B: take
17. was combing . . . broke . . . finished . . . rushed
18. get . . . 'm/am going to read / I will read . . . watch . . . 'm/am not going to do / won't do

20. A: has . . . has
    B: does she have
    B: Do you have
    A: 'm/am not going to get . . . don't have

Chapter 4: THE PRESENT PERFECT AND THE PAST PERFECT

◇ PRACTICE 1, p. 64.

1. A: Have you ever eaten
   B: have . . . have eaten OR haven't . . . have never eaten
2. A: Have you ever talked
   B: have . . . have talked OR haven't . . . have never talked
3. A: Has Erica ever rented
   B: has . . . has rented OR hasn't . . . has never rented
4. A: Have you ever seen
   B: have . . . have seen OR haven't . . . have never seen
5. A: Has Joe ever caught
   B: has . . . has caught OR hasn't . . . has never caught
6. A: Have you ever had
   B: have . . . have had OR haven't . . . have never had

◇ PRACTICE 2, p. 65.

1. have wanted
2. have been
3. has been
4. have flown
5. have not picked up
6. has changed
7. has already corrected . . . hasn't returned
8. hasn't talked
9. have needed . . . have looked
10. A: Have you had
    B: have gotten

◇ PRACTICE 3, p. 66.

GROUP I.

simple form	simple past	past participle
hurt	hurt	hurt
put	put	put
quit	quit	quit
upset	upset	upset
cut	cut	cut
shut	shut	shut
let	let	let
set	set	set

GROUP II.

simple form	simple past	past participle
ring	rang	rung
drink	drank	drunk
swim	swam	swum
sing	sang	sung
sink	sank	sunk

GROUP III.

simple form	simple past	past participle
win	won	won
feed	fed	fed
weep	wept	wept
stand	stood	stood
keep	kept	kept
sit	sat	sat
stick	stuck	stuck
meet	met	met
have	had	had
find	found	found
buy	bought	bought
catch	caught	caught
fight	fought	fought
teach	taught	taught
pay	paid	paid
bring	brought	brought
think	thought	thought

◇ PRACTICE 4, p. 67.

1. have used
2. has risen
3. have never played
4. have won
5. hasn't spoken
6. hasn't eaten
7. has given
8. haven't saved
9. Have you ever slept
10. have never worn
11. has improved
12. have looked

◇ PRACTICE 5, p. 68.

1. C	6. F	11. F
2. F	7. F	12. F
3. F	8. F	13. F
4. F	9. C	14. C
5. C	10. C	

◇ PRACTICE 6, p. 68.

1. began . . . have begun
2. bent . . . have bent
3. broadcast . . . has broadcast
4. caught . . . have caught
5. came . . . have come
6. cut . . . have cut
7. dug . . . have dug
8. drew . . . has drawn
9. fed . . . have fed
10. fought . . . have fought
11. forgot . . . have forgotten
12. hid . . . have hidden
13. hit . . . has hit
14. held . . . has held
15. kept . . . have kept
16. led . . . has led
17. lost . . . has lost
18. met . . . have met
19. rode . . . have ridden
20. rang . . . has rung
21. saw . . . have seen
22. stole . . . has stolen
23. stuck . . . have stuck
24. swept . . . have swept
25. took . . . have taken
26. upset . . . have upset
27. withdrew . . . have withdrawn
28. wrote . . . have written

◇ PRACTICE 7, p. 70.

1. went . . . have gone
2. lived
3. has lived
4. moved . . . worked
5. roomed . . . returned
6. was . . . died
7. has played
8. has not/hasn't slept
9. made
10. have enjoyed
11. collected

◇ PRACTICE 8, p. 71.

1. a. have gone
   b. went
2. a. gave
   b. Has she ever given
3. a. have fallen
   b. fell
4. a. Have you ever broken
   b. broke
5. a. have never shaken
   b. shook
6. a. heard
   b. have heard
7. a. flew
   b. has flown
8. a. has worn
   b. wore
9. a. Have you ever built
   b. built
10. a. has taught
    b. taught
11. a. have you ever found
    b. found
12. a. drove
    b. have never driven
13. a. sang
    b. have sung
14. a. have never run
    b. ran
15. a. told
    b. has told
16. a. stood
    b. have stood
17. a. spent
    b. have already spent
18. a. have made
    b. made
19. a. has risen
    b. rose
20. a. felt
    b. have felt

◇ PRACTICE 9, p. 73.

1. since	6. since	11. for
2. for	7. since	12. for
3. since	8. for	13. since
4. for	9. since	14. for
5. for	10. since	

◇ PRACTICE 10, p. 74.

1. I have been in this class **for** a month.
2. I have known my teacher **since** September.
3. Sam has wanted a dog **for** two years.
4. Sara has needed a new car **since** last year / **for** a year.
5. Our professor has been sick **for** a week / **since** last week.
6. They have lived in Canada **since** December.
7. I have known Mrs. Brown **since** 1999.
8. Tom has worked at a fast-food restaurant **for** three weeks.

◇ PRACTICE 11, p. 74.

Checked phrases:
1. two weeks ago
   yesterday
   last year
   several months ago
   the day before yesterday
   in March
2. since Friday
   since last week
   for several weeks

◇ PRACTICE 12, p. 75.

1. have known . . . was
2. has had . . . came
3. have not experienced . . . came
4. began . . . has given
5. has been . . . was
6. has not been . . . graduated
7. started . . . have completed
8. began . . . has not had
9. have become . . . changed
10. has risen . . . bought

10 ANSWER KEY Chapter 4

◇ PRACTICE 13, p. 75.
1. A: has Eric been studying
   B: 's been studying . . . for two hours
2. A: has Kathy been working at the computer
   B: 's been working . . . two o'clock
3. A: has it been raining
   B: 's been raining . . . two days
4. A: has Liz been reading
   B: 's been reading . . . 30 minutes/half an hour
5. A: has Boris been studying English
   B: 's been studying English . . . 2001
6. A: has Nicole been working at the Silk Road Clothing Store
   B: 's been working . . . three months
7. A: has Ms. Rice been teaching at this school
   B: 's been teaching . . . 2001
8. A: has Mr. Fisher been driving a Chevy
   B: 's been driving a Chevy . . . twelve years
9. A: has Mrs. Taylor been waiting to see her doctor
   B: 's been waiting . . . one and a half hours
10. A: have Ted and Erica been playing tennis
    B: have been playing tennis . . . two o'clock

◇ PRACTICE 14, p. 76.
1. B   4. B   7. B
2. B   5. A   8. A
3. A   6. A

◇ PRACTICE 15, p. 77.
1. B   5. C   9. B
2. D   6. A   10. C
3. A   7. C
4. D   8. D

◇ PRACTICE 16, p. 78.
1. yet   11. A: yet
2. yet   B: still
3. still   12. yet . . . still
4. yet   13. already
5. still   14. still
6. still   15. anymore
7. yet   16. still
8. still   17. already
9. anymore   18. yet . . . still
10. still

◇ PRACTICE 17, p. 79.
1. need   13. don't have
2. is   14. haven't had
3. Have you ever worked   15. quit
4. have worked   16. Are you looking
5. had   17. 'm/am going
6. did you work   18. is looking
7. have worked   19. 'll/will do
8. have never had   20. have never looked
9. did you like   21. 'll/will be (also possible: is)
10. didn't like   22. don't know
11. was   23. 'll/will find
12. are you working   24. go

◇ PRACTICE 18, p. 80.
1. have already eaten   5. had already finished
2. had already eaten   6. had already started
3. have already finished   7. has already started
4. had already finished   8. had already left

◇ PRACTICE 19, p. 81.
1. was raining
2. had stopped
3. was studying
4. had finished
5. was washing
6. had already washed . . . (had) put

◇ PRACTICE 20, p. 82.
Past perfect verbs:
(1) had always watched
(2) had always read
(3) had never let . . . had always listened
(4) had always left
(5) 'd/had never put
(6) had never shared

1. had always watched
2. had always read
3. had never let
4. had always left
5. had never put
6. had never shared

◇ PRACTICE 21, p. 83.
1. A: Did you enjoy
   B: hadn't gone
2. A: Did you see
   B: was . . . hadn't seen
3. A: haven't seen
   B: is . . . haven't seen
4. A: Did you get
   B: got . . . had already begun
5. had already gone
6. have painted
7. A: was watching
   B: did you do
   A: ran
8. A: Did you go
   B: got . . . had already made
   A: was
   B: had . . . were eating . . . stopped . . . invited

◇ PRACTICE 22, p. 84.
1. Where have you been? I've **been** waiting for you for an hour.
2. Anna **has** been a soccer fan **for** a long time.
3. Since I **was** a child, I **have** liked to solve puzzles.
4. Have you ever **wanted** to travel around the world?
5. The family **has been** at the hospital since they **heard** about the accident.
6. My sister is only 30 years old, but her hair has **begun** to turn gray.
7. Jake has **worked** as a volunteer at the children's hospital several times.

8. Steve has worn his black suit only once since he ~~has~~ bought it.
9. My cousin **has been** studying for medical school exams since last month.
10. The students **have been** hearing rumors about their teacher's engagement for a week.
11. I don't know the results of my medical tests **yet**. I'll find out soon.
12. Jean has been **trying** to get online to go Internet shopping for an hour.
13. By the time Michelle unlocked the door and got into her apartment, the phone **had** already stopped ringing.

Chapter 5: ASKING QUESTIONS

◇ PRACTICE 1, p. 85.
1. (*your name*)
2. what is your name
3. Is that your first name?
4. What's your last name?
5. How do you spell it?
6. Where are you from?
7. What is your hometown?
8. When did you come here?
9. Why did you come here?
10. What are you studying? (OR What is your major?)
11. How long are you going to stay here?
12. Where are you living?
13. Is it far from school?
14. How far is it?
15. How do you get to school?
16. Do you like it?

◇ PRACTICE 2, p. 86.

helping verb	subject	main verb	rest of sentence
1. Do	you	like	coffee?
2. Does	Tom	like	coffee?
3. Is	Ann	watching	TV?
4. Are	you	having	lunch with Rob?
5. Did	Sara	walk	to school?
6. Was	Ann	taking	a nap?
7. Will	Ted	come	to the meeting?
8. Can	Rita	ride	a bicycle?

form of **be**	subject	rest of sentence
9. Is	Ann	a good artist?
10. Were	you	at the wedding?

◇ PRACTICE 3, p. 87.
1. A: Do
   B: I don't
2. A: Is
   B: it isn't
3. A: Do
   B: they do
4. A: Are
   B: I am
5. A: Are
   B: they aren't
6. A: Do
   B: they do
7. A: Is
   B: it isn't
8. A: Does
   B: it doesn't
9. A: Are
   B: I am
10. A: Does
    B: it does

◇ PRACTICE 4, p. 88.
1. Yes, I do. OR No, I don't.
2. Yes, she does. OR No she doesn't.
3. Yes, I am. OR No, I'm not.
4. Yes, I will. OR No, I won't.
5. Yes, I can. OR No, I can't.
6. Yes, I do. OR No, I don't.
7. Yes, we are. OR No, we aren't.
8. Yes, they can. OR No, they can't.
9. Yes, they should. OR No, they shouldn't.
10. Yes, I did. OR No, I didn't.
11. Yes, I do. OR No, I don't.
12. Yes, it will. OR No, it won't.
13. Yes, it does. OR No, it doesn't.
14. Yes, they were. OR No, they weren't.
15. Yes, he/she should. OR No, he/she shouldn't.
16. Yes, it is. OR No, it isn't.
17. Yes, it was. OR No, it wasn't.

◇ PRACTICE 5, p. 89.
1. A: Does Jane eat
   B: she does.
2. A: Do
   B: they don't.
3. A: Did Ann and Jim come
   B: they didn't.
4. A: Are you writing
   B: I am.
5. A: Were you
   B: I wasn't.
6. A: Is Tim Wilson
   B: he is.
7. A: Will Karen finish
   B: she will.
8. A: Can birds swim
   B: they can.
9. A: Have you looked
   B: I haven't.

◇ PRACTICE 6, p. 89.

question word	helping verb	subject	main verb	rest of sentence
1. Ø	Did	you	hear	the news yesterday?
2. When	did	you	hear	the news?
3. Ø	Is	Eric	reading	today's paper?
4. What	is	Eric	reading?	Ø
5. Ø	Did	you	find	your wallet?
6. Where	did	you	find	your wallet?
7. Why	does	Mr. Li	walk	to work?
8. Ø	Does	Mr. Li	walk	to work?
9. Ø	Will	Ms. Cook	return	to her office?
10. When	will	Ms. Cook	return	to her office?
11. Ø	Is	the orange juice		in the refrigerator?
12. Where	is	the orange juice?		Ø

◇ PRACTICE 7, p. 90.

1. What time/When do the fireworks start
2. Why are you waiting
3. When does Rachel start
4. What time/When do you leave
5. Why didn't you get
6. Where can I find
7. When are you leaving
8. When do you expect
9. Where will the spaceship go
10. Where did you study . . . Why did you study . . . Why didn't you go

◇ PRACTICE 8, p. 91.

1. When/What time did you get up
2. Where did you eat lunch
3. When/What time did you eat
4. Why do you eat lunch
5. Where do your aunt and uncle live
6. When are you going to visit
7. When/What time will you get home
8. Where is George going to study
9. Why does George study
10. Where can I catch
11. When/What time do you have to leave
12. Where were you living
13. Why are the students writing
14. What time should I call
15. Why is Yoko

◇ PRACTICE 9, p. 92.

1. were you
2. can't you come
3. did Tom go
4. won't Ann be
5. do you need
6. are you going to buy
7. didn't you do
8. isn't Anita coming
9. are you and Joe going
10. didn't you eat
11. did Jack take
12. don't you like

◇ PRACTICE 10, p. 93.

1. Who knows Tom?
2. Who(m) does Tom know?
3. Who will help us?
4. Who(m) will you ask?
5. Who(m) is Eric talking to on the phone? OR (formal: To whom is Eric talking on the phone?)
6. Who is knocking on the door?
7. What surprised them?
8. What did Jack say?
9. What did Sue talk about?
10. Who(m) did Ann talk about? OR (formal: About whom did Ann talk?)

◇ PRACTICE 11, p. 94.

1. Who taught
2. What did Robert see
3. Who got
4. What are you making
5. Who does that calculator belong
6. What do you have
7. What did the cat kill
8. What killed the cat
9. What makes
10. Who wrote a note
11. Who(m) did you get a letter

◇ PRACTICE 12, p. 95.

1. A: What does "explore" mean?
   B: "to go to a new place and find out about it."
2. A: What does "underneath" mean?
   B: "under."
3. A: What does "blink" mean?
   B: "to open and close your eyes quickly."
4. A: What does "delicious" mean?
   B: "it tastes very, very, good."

◇ PRACTICE 13, p. 95.

1. What is Alex doing?
2. What should I do
3. What do astronauts do?
4. What are you going to do
5. What do you do
6. What can I do
7. What did Sara do
8. What should I do?
9. What is Emily going to do
10. What did you do
11. What would you like to do (also possible: Where would you like to go)
12. What are you trying to do?
13. What does Kevin need to do?
14. What does Nick do?
15. What did he do? . . . What did you do? . . . what did he do?

◇ PRACTICE 14, p. 96.

1. What kind of music
2. What kind of clothes/clothing
3. What kind of food
4. What kind of books
5. What kind of car
6. What kind of government
7. What kind of job
8. What kind of person/man/woman
9. What kind of products/things

◇ PRACTICE 15, p. 97.

1. Which
2. What
3. Which
4. What
5. Which
6. Which
7. What
8. What
9. Which

◇ PRACTICE 16, p. 98.

1. Who
2. Whose
3. Whose
4. Who
5. Who
6. Who
7. Whose
8. Whose

◇ PRACTICE 17, p. 99.

1. Whose house is that?
2. Who's living in that house?
3. Whose umbrella did you borrow?
4. Whose book did you use?
5. Whose book is on the table?
6. Who is on the phone?
7. Who's that?
8. Whose is that?

◇ PRACTICE 18, p. 99.
1. A: hot
   B: hot
2. soon
3. expensive
4. A: busy
   B: busy
5. A: serious
   B: serious
6. safe
7. B: fresh
   A: fresh . . . fresh
8. A: well
   B: well

◇ PRACTICE 19, p. 100.
1. far	7. long	13. long
2. long	8. far	14. often
3. often	9. long	15. far
4. far	10. often	16. long
5. far	11. long	17. often
6. often	12. far	

◇ PRACTICE 20, p. 101.
1. What is Jack doing
2. Who is he playing
3. What is Anna doing
4. What is she throwing
5. What are Anna and Jack holding
6. What is
7. Where are they
8. How long have they been playing
9. Who is winning
10. Who won

◇ PRACTICE 21, p. 102.
1. When will the clean clothes be
2. Where did you go
3. Which dictionary did you buy
4. How long did it take you
5. How can I reach
6. What kind of bread do you like
7. Why didn't you answer
8. Who are you going
9. Who repaired
10. How is the weather

◇ PRACTICE 22, p. 103.
1. a. don't	c. is
b. doesn't	d. weren't
c. don't	e. was
d. doesn't	4. a. hasn't
e. isn't	b. haven't
f. aren't	c. have
g. does	d. hasn't
h. is	e. has
2. a. didn't	5. a. can't
b. did	b. will
c. were	c. shouldn't
d. wasn't	d. wouldn't
3. a. aren't	e. do
b. is	f. didn't

◇ PRACTICE 23, p. 104.
1. A: haven't you?	9. A: doesn't he?
B: Yes, I have.	B: Yes, he does.
2. A: has he?	10. A: didn't you?
B: No, he hasn't.	B: Yes, I did.
3. A: didn't you?	11. A: is it?
B: Yes, I did.	B: No, it isn't.
4. A: don't you?	12. A: does he?
B: Yes, I do.	B: No, he doesn't.
5. A: haven't they?	13. A: do I?
B: Yes, they have.	B: No, you don't.
6. A: hasn't she?	14. A: is it?
B: Yes, she has.	B: No, it isn't.
7. A: is it?	15. A: weren't they?
B: No, it isn't.	B: Yes, they were.
8. A: don't we?	16. A: will she?
B: Yes, we do.	B: No, she won't.

◇ PRACTICE 24, p. 105.
1. **Who** saw the car accident?
2. Why **didn't you** say "good-bye" when you left?
3. How about **asking** Julie and Tim to come for dinner Friday night?
4. What time **does** class **begin** today?
5. Why **does** he have no shoes on his feet?
   (*also possible:* Why **doesn't** he have **any** shoes on his feet?)
6. Where **can you** get a drink of water in this building?
7. What kind of music **do** you like best?
8. How long **does** it **take** to get to the beach from here?
9. She is working late tonight, **isn't** she?
10. **Whose** glasses are those?
11. How ~~much~~ tall **is** your father?
12. Who **did** you **talk** to about registration for next term?
13. How about ~~we~~ **going** to see the baby elephant at the zoo tomorrow?
14. How far **is it** from here to the nearest gas station?

◇ PRACTICE 25, p. 106.
1. When are you going to buy
2. How are you going to pay
3. How long did you have
4. How often do you ride
5. How do you get
6. Are you going to ride
7. Why didn't you ride
8. Does your bike have
9. What kind of bike do you have
10. When did Jason get
11. Who broke
12. What did Billy break
13. Whose new bike is broken
14. How did Billy break
15. Which bicycle is
16. Where do you keep
17. Who does that bike belong to
18. Whose bike did you borrow
19. Where is Rita
20. What is she doing
21. How far did Rita ride
22. How do you spell

Chapter 6: NOUNS AND PRONOUNS

◇ PRACTICE 1, p. 108.

1. Airplanes . . . wings
2. Children . . . swings
3. animals . . . zoos
4. Trees . . . branches . . . leaves
5. ducks . . . geese . . . pond . . . park
6. babies . . . teeth
7. potatoes . . . beans . . . peas . . . tomatoes
8. Opinions . . . facts
9. country . . . customs
10. Governments . . . taxes

◇ PRACTICE 2, p. 108.

1. /z/   7. /əz/
2. /s/   8. /z/
3. /s/   9. /s/
4. /əz/   10. /əz/
5. /z/   11. /z/
6. /z/   12. /s/

◇ PRACTICE 3, p. 108.

1. /z/   7. /z/
2. /s/   8. /s/
3. /əz/   9. /əz/
4. /s/   10. /s/
5. /z/   11. /əz/
6. /z/   12. /əz/

◇ PRACTICE 4, p. 109.

1. /z/ . . . /z/ . . . /z/
2. /əz/ . . . /əz/
3. /z/ . . . /z/ . . . /z/
4. /əz/ . . . /z/
5. /z/ . . . /əz/
6. /z/ . . . /əz/ . . . /s/
7. /əz/ . . . /əz/
8. /z/ . . . /z/ . . . /z/

◇ PRACTICE 5, p. 109.

1. mouse   12. beliefs   23. sheep
2. pockets   13. potatoes   24. loaf
3. tooth   14. radios   25. glasses
4. tomato   15. offspring   26. problems
5. fish   16. child   27. families
6. woman   17. seasons   28. wives
7. branches   18. customs   29. shelves
8. friends   19. businesses   30. roofs
9. duties   20. century   31. foot
10. highways   21. occurrences   32. women
11. thieves   22. phenomenon

◇ PRACTICE 6, p. 110.

1. cows, sheep, horses, mice, geese
2. potatoes, tomatoes, peas, beans
3. apples, grapes, strawberries, bananas, cherries, pears
4. poppies, daffodils, roses, daisies, lilies
5. babies, sons, daughters, husbands, wives, children

◇ PRACTICE 7, p. 111.

1. Children(S) play(V) games(O).
2. Fish(S) swim(V).
3. The baby(S) doesn't like(V) her new toys(O).
4. Computers(S) process(V) information(O) quickly.
5. Dictionaries(S) give(V) definitions(O).
6. Teachers(S) correct(V) tests(O).
7. The cat(S) found(V) a mouse(O).
8. The sun(S) shines(V) brightly.
9. Water(S) evaporates(V).
10. Do(V) snakes(S) lay(V) eggs(O)?
11. The child(S) petted(V) the dog(O).
12. Did(V) the phone(S) ring(V)?

◇ PRACTICE 8, p. 111.

1. The man opened the door with(PREP) his key(O of PREP).
2. The little girl put her shoes on(PREP) the wrong feet(O of PREP).
3. The student added and subtracted with(PREP) a calculator(O of PREP).
4. My father fixes breakfast for(PREP) my mother(O of PREP) every morning.
5. Librarians work in(PREP) libraries(O of PREP).
6. The bird flew into(PREP) the window(O of PREP) of(PREP) the building(O of PREP).
7. I do all my homework on(PREP) a computer(O of PREP).
8. The artist drew scenes of(PREP) the beach(O of PREP) in(PREP) his notebook(O of PREP).
9. The children played in(PREP) the backyard(O of PREP) until(PREP) dinner(O of PREP).
10. It rained for(PREP) two weeks(O of PREP).
11. The painter splashed paint on(PREP) the floor(O of PREP) of(PREP) his studio(O of PREP).
12. A man with(PREP) dark glasses(O of PREP) stood near(PREP) the door(O of PREP).

◇ PRACTICE 9, p. 112.

1. <u>Bridges</u> <u>cross</u> <u>rivers</u>.
   (S / V / O)
2. <u>A terrible earthquake</u> <u>occurred</u> <u>in Turkey</u>.
   (S / V / PP)
3. <u>Airplanes</u> <u>fly</u> <u>above the clouds</u>.
   (S / V / PP)
4. <u>Trucks</u> <u>carry</u> large <u>loads</u>.
   (S / V / O)
5. <u>Rivers</u> <u>flow</u> <u>toward the sea</u>.
   (S / V / PP)
6. <u>Salespeople</u> <u>treat</u> <u>customers</u> <u>with courtesy</u>.
   (S / V / O / PP)
7. <u>Bacteria</u> <u>can cause</u> <u>diseases</u>.
   (S / V / O)
8. <u>Clouds</u> <u>are floating</u> <u>across the sky</u>.
   (S / V / PP)
9. <u>The audience</u> <u>in the theater</u> <u>applauded</u> <u>the performers</u>
   <u>at the end</u> <u>of the show</u>.
   (S / PP / V / O / PP / PP)
10. <u>Helmets</u> <u>protect</u> <u>bicyclists</u> <u>from serious injuries</u>.
    (S / V / O / PP)

◇ PRACTICE 10, p. 112.

1. in	5. at	9. at	13. in
2. in	6. at	10. at	14. in
3. on	7. in	11. in	15. on
4. on	8. on	12. on	

◇ PRACTICE 11, p. 113.

1. 3	4. 2	7. 2
1	1	3
2	3	1
2. 1	5. 1	8. 3
2	3	1
3	2	2
3. 2	6. 3	9. 2
3	1	1
1	2	3

◇ PRACTICE 12, p. 114.

1. are	5. is	9. are
2. are	6. is	10. is
3. are	7. is	
4. is	8. is	

◇ PRACTICE 13, p. 114.

1. make	5. are	9. needs
2. need	6. comes	10. go
3. Do	7. is	11. work
4. are	8. are	12. are

◇ PRACTICE 14, p. 114.

1. old	9. hard	17. cheap/inexpensive
2. old	10. narrow	18. light
3. cold/cool	11. clean	19. light
4. slow	12. empty	20. public
5. happy	13. safe	21. right
6. bad	14. noisy	22. right
7. wet	15. deep	23. strong
8. easy	16. sour	24. long

◇ PRACTICE 15, p. 115.

adjective	→	noun it describes
1. loud	→	voice
2. sweet	→	Sugar
3. easy	→	test
4. free	→	Air
5. delicious	→	food
Mexican	→	restaurant
6. important	→	facts
wide	→	variety
7. sick	→	child
8. sick	→	child
warm	→	bed
hot	→	tea
9. camping	→	equipment
old, rusty	→	equipment
10. hungry	→	bear
garbage	→	cans
11. elderly	→	father
nursing	→	care
12. fresh	→	coffee
warm	→	cookies

◇ PRACTICE 16, p. 116.

1. newspaper articles	11. brick walls
2. page numbers	12. egg cartons
3. paper money	13. mountain views
4. apartment buildings	14. pocket knives
5. computer disks	15. traffic lights
6. birthday presents	16. picnic tables
7. rose gardens	17. apple pies
8. key chains	18. bicycle helmets
9. city governments	19. log cabins
10. duck ponds	20. steel bridges

◇ PRACTICE 17, p. 117.

1. mountains
2. Cats . . . **mice**
3. Mosquito**es**/Mosquit**os** . . . insect**s**
4. eyelash**es**
5. Gee**se** . . . ducks
6. programs
7. Forest**s** . . . fire**s** . . . fire**s** . . . animals
8. kni**ves** . . . weapons
9. manners
10. tickets
11. li**ves** . . . way**s** . . . year**s** . . . lamp**s** . . . candle**s** . . . house**s** . . . chicken**s** . . . fire**s**
12. kind**s** . . . flowers
13. reporter**s** . . . jobs
14. universi**ties**
15. students
16. animal**s** . . . horse**s** . . . zebra**s** [NOTE: *deer* is already plural]
17. student**s** . . . experiment**s** . . . class**es**
18. House**flies** . . . pest**s** . . . germs
19. article**s** . . . experiences
20. device**s** . . . batter**ies** . . . flashlight**s** . . . calculator**s** . . . radio**s** . . . recorder**s** . . . kind**s** . . . toy**s** . . . batter**ies**

◇ PRACTICE 18, p. 118

1. The teacher helped _me_ [O of V] with the lesson.
2. I [S] carry a dictionary with _me_ [O of PREP] at all times.
3. Mr. Fong has a computer. He [S] uses _it_ [O of V] for many things. It [S] helps _him_ [O of V] in many ways.
4. Jessica went to Hawaii with Ann and _me_ [O of PREP]. We [S] like _her_ [O of V], and she [S] likes _us_ [O of V]. We [S] had a good time with _her_ [O of PREP].
5. Mike had dirty socks. He [S] washed _them_ [O of V] in the kitchen sink and hung _them_ [O of V] to dry in front of the window. They [S] dried quickly.
6. Joseph and I [S] are close friends. No bad feelings will ever come between _him_ [O of PREP] and _me_ [O of PREP]. He [S] and I [S] share a strong bond of friendship.

◇ PRACTICE 19, p. 118.

	pronoun	→	noun/noun phrase
1.	She	→	Janet
	it	→	a green apple
2.	her	→	Betsy
3.	They	→	Nick and Rob
4.	They	→	phone messages
5.	him	→	Louie
	He	→	Louie
	her	→	Alice
	She	→	Alice
6.	She	→	Jane
	it	→	letter
	them	→	Mr. and Mrs. Moore
	They	→	Mr. and Mrs. Moore
	her	→	Jane

◇ PRACTICE 20, p. 119.

1. me
2. He
3. him
4. he
5. her
6. She
7. me . . . He . . . us
8. her . . . They
9. I . . . They . . . us . . . it . . . We . . . them
10. them
11. me . . . him
12. she
13. I . . . him and me
14. them . . . They . . . her . . . it . . . She
15. me . . . him
16. me . . . him
17. me . . . he . . . him . . . us . . . We . . . We . . . him . . . he

◇ PRACTICE 21, p. 120.

1. friend's
2. friends'
3. son's
4. sons'
5. baby's
6. babies'
7. child's
8. children's
9. person's
10. people's
11. teacher's
12. teachers'
13. man's
14. men's
15. earth's

◇ PRACTICE 22, p. 120.

1. Dan's
2. (no change)
3. Jack's
4. (no change)
5. roommate's
6. roommates'
7. (no change)
8. Betty's . . . sister's
9. sisters'
10. woman's
11. women's . . . men's
12. Jupiter's surface
13. Mercury's atmosphere
14. Mars'/Mars's surface . . . Earth's surface
15. Earth's twin . . . Venus'/Venus's surface
16. planets' . . . Jupiter's son . . . Venus'/Venus's son

◇ PRACTICE 23, p. 122.

1. your . . . yours
2. her . . . hers
3. his . . . his
4. your . . . yours
5. their . . . our . . . theirs . . . ours

◇ PRACTICE 24, p. 122.

1. her
2. hers
3. Our
4. Ours
5. your
6. mine . . . my . . . yours
7. their . . . theirs
8. mine . . . yours
9. ours

◇ PRACTICE 25, p. 123.

1. myself
2. himself
3. ourselves
4. yourself
5. yourselves
6. herself
7. themselves
8. himself
9. herself
10. myself
11. ourselves
12. themselves
13. herself/himself
14. ourselves
15. themselves
16. herself
17. himself
18. themselves
19. yourself/yourselves

◇ PRACTICE 26, p. 124.

1. cut myself
2. be proud of yourself
3. talks to himself
4. taught myself
5. blamed herself
6. help yourselves
7. takes care of himself
8. enjoyed themselves
9. worked for himself
10. introduce themselves

◇ PRACTICE 27, p. 125.

1. me . . . him
2. yourselves
3. itself
4. its . . . its
5. hers
6. him
7. yourself . . . your
8. our . . . our
9. ours
10. themselves
11. itself
12. himself

◇ PRACTICE 28, p. 125.

1. his . . . He . . . himself . . . he . . . him
2. Her . . . She
3. Our . . . We
4. her
5. my . . . I
6. hers
7. mine

8. They . . . themselves . . . them . . . theirs . . . Their . . . their
9. hers . . . his
10. himself . . . him . . . he . . . his . . . He . . . him
11. her . . . she . . . herself *(also possible:* it*)* . . . she . . . her
12. your . . . ours

◇ PRACTICE 29, p. 126.
1. one . . . another . . . another . . . the other
2. one . . . another . . . the other
3. one . . . another . . . another . . . another . . . the other
4. one . . . the other
5. one . . . another . . . another . . . another . . . another . . . the other

◇ PRACTICE 30, p. 127.
1. another
2. The other
3. The other
4. Another
5. The other
6. a. Another
   b. the other
7. a. another
   b. another
c. another
d. another
e. another
8. another
9. The other
10. The other
11. another

◇ PRACTICE 31, p. 128.
1. The others
2. The others
3. Others
4. others
5. other
6. Others
7. Other
8. Others
9. Other
10. The others
11. The other
12. The other
13. Others . . . other
14. another . . . other
15. another . . . Other
16. The others
17. The other

◇ PRACTICE 32, p. 129.
1. A
2. C
3. D
4. B
5. B
6. A
7. D
8. B

◇ PRACTICE 33, p. 130.
1. are
2. potatoes
3. by myself
4. on . . . at
5. four-week
6. us
7. its
8. our . . . yours
9. himself
10. the others

◇ PRACTICE 34, p. 130.
1. Look at those **beautiful** mountains!
2. The children played **a game at the park** on Saturday afternoon.
3. There are two **horses**, several **sheep**, and a cow in the **farmer's** field.
4. The owner of the store is busy **at** the moment.
5. The teacher met **her** students at the park after school.
6. Everyone **wants** peace in the world.
7. I grew up in a **very large** city.
8. This apple tastes sour. Here's some more, so let's try **another** (OR **another one**).

9. Some **trees** lose their **leaves** in the winter.
10. I am going to wear my **brown** shirt ~~is~~ to the party.
11. I hurt **myself** at work last week.
12. Our neighbors invited my friend and **me** to visit **them**.
13. My **husband's** boss works for twelve **hours** every **day**.
14. The students couldn't find **their** books.
15. I always read **magazine** articles while I'm in the waiting room at my **dentist's** office.

Chapter 7: MODAL AUXILIARIES

◇ PRACTICE 1, p. 132.
(1) has to = *must*
(3) can't = *is not able to*
    may = *might*
(5) couldn't = *was not able to*
(7) got to = *must*
(10) have to = *must*
(12) 'd (had) better = *should*
(13) ought to = *should*
    has to = *must*
(17) might = *may*
(21) ought to = *should*

◇ PRACTICE 2, p. 133.
1. Ø
2. to
3. Ø
4. Ø
5. Ø
6. to
7. Ø
8. to
9. Ø
10. Ø . . . Ø
11. to . . . Ø
12. Ø
13. Ø

◇ PRACTICE 3, p. 134.
1. zebra
2. cat
3. Elephants
4. Monkeys
5. camels
6. cow
7. horse
8. donkey
9. squirrel
10. ants
11. baby
12. women

◇ PRACTICE 4, p. 134.
1. may/might . . . may not/might not
2. can't
3. can . . . may/might . . . may not/might not
4. may/might
5. can't
6. may/might . . . may/might
7. can't

◇ PRACTICE 5, p. 135.
1. I might take a nap.
2. Maybe she is sick.
3. Maybe there will be time later.
4. Our team may win.
5. You might be right.
6. We may hear soon.
7. It may rain.
8. It might snow.
9. Maybe she will come tomorrow.
10. Maybe she is at home right now.

◇ PRACTICE 6, p. 135.
1. possibility
2. possibility
3. permission
4. possibility
5. possibility
6. permission
7. possibility
8. permission
9. possibility
10. permission

◇ PRACTICE 7, p. 136.
1. b
2. b
3. a
4. a
5. b
6. a
7. b
8. a

◇ PRACTICE 8, p. 137.
1. Can
2. may
3. Would
4. could
5. Can
6. A: Could
   B: May
7. A: Can
   B: Will
8. Could

◇ PRACTICE 9, p. 137.
1. Could/Can/Would
2. Could/May/Can
3. Would/Could/Will
4. Can/May/Could
5. Will/Can/Could

◇ PRACTICE 10, p. 138.
1. shouldn't drive a long distance
2. should quit
3. shouldn't exceed the speed limit
4. shouldn't give too much homework
5. shouldn't miss any classes
6. shouldn't be cruel to animals
7. should always be on time for an appointment
8. shouldn't throw trash out of your car window

◇ PRACTICE 11, p. 138.
1. soak it in cold water . . . wash it in hot water
2. take it back to the store . . . try to fix it herself
3. get a job
4. call the landlord and complain
5. find a new girlfriend
6. send it back to the kitchen . . . eat it

◇ PRACTICE 12, p. 139.
1. A
2. C
3. B
4. A
5. B
6. C
7. A
8. C
9. B
10. C

◇ PRACTICE 13, p. 140.
1. C
2. A
3. D
4. C
5. B
6. A
7. D
8. C

◇ PRACTICE 14, p. 140.
1. have to/must
2. had to
3. have to/must
4. had to
5. has to
6. had to
7. have to/must
8. had to

◇ PRACTICE 15, p. 141.
1. had to
2. had to
3. have to
4. had to
5. have to
6. had to

◇ PRACTICE 16, p. 141.
1. had to study
2. had to turn off
3. Did you have to work
4. had to see
5. had to be
6. had to close

◇ PRACTICE 17, p. 141.
1. must not
2. don't have to
3. don't have to
4. don't have to
5. must not
6. don't have to
7. must not
8. must not
9. must not
10. don't have to
11. don't have to
12. must not
13. must not
14. must not
15. don't have to

◇ PRACTICE 18, p. 143.
1. must/have to
2. doesn't have to
3. don't have to
4. must/has to
5. doesn't have to
6. must/has to
7. must not

◇ PRACTICE 19, p. 143.
People have to/must . . .
eat and drink in order to live
pay taxes
stop when they see a police car's lights behind them

People must not . . .
fall asleep while driving
drive without a license
take other people's belongings

People don't have to . . .
cook every meal themselves
say "sir" or "madam" to others
stay in their homes in the evening

◇ PRACTICE 20, p. 144.
1. 2
2. 1
3. 1
4. 2
5. 1
6. 2
7. 2
8. 2
9. 1

◇ PRACTICE 21, p. 144.
1. Wait
2. Don't wait
3. Read
4. Don't put
5. Come . . . have
6. Don't cross
7. Don't stand . . . Do
8. Call
9. Take . . . Go . . . Walk . . . give
10. Capitalize . . . Put . . . use

◇ PRACTICE 22, p. 145.
1. 1
   4
   3
   2
2. 2
   1
   4
   3
3. 2
   1
4. 4
   2
   1
   3

◇ PRACTICE 23, p. 145.

1. A: go . . . fly
   B: see
2. A: get
   B: take/ask
3. A: go
   B: play
4. A: get/take
   B: take . . . save
5. A: stop . . . fill up
   B: get/pick up
6. go . . . call . . . ask/see

◇ PRACTICE 24, p. 146.

1. prefer
2. like
3. would rather
4. prefer
5. would rather
6. A: prefer
   B: likes . . . would rather
7. would rather
8. would rather
9. B: prefer
   A: like
10. prefer

◇ PRACTICE 25, p. 147.

1. Kim prefers salad to dessert.
2. In general, Nicole likes coffee better than tea.
3. Bill would rather teach history than work as a business executive.
4. When considering a pet, Sam likes dogs better than cats.
5. On a long trip, Susie prefers to drive than (to) ride in the back seat.
6. I would rather study in a noisy room than study in a completely quiet room.
7. Alex would rather play soccer than baseball.

◇ PRACTICE 26, p. 148.

1. C	6. C	11. B
2. A	7. B	12. B
3. C	8. C	13. A
4. A	9. B	14. C
5. B	10. C	15. A

◇ PRACTICE 27, p. 149.

1. Before I left on my trip last month, I **had to** get a passport.
2. Could you ~~to~~ bring us more coffee, please?
3. Ben can **drive**, but he prefers **to** take the bus.
4. My roommate **may be** at home this evening.
5. A few of our classmates can't ~~to~~ come to the school picnic.
6. **Could/Would/Will/Can** you take our picture, please?
7. Jane's eyes are red, and she is yawning. She must **be** sleepy.
8. Jim would rather **have** Fridays off in the summer than **have/take** a long vacation.
9. I must **read** several lengthy books for my literature class.
10. Take your warm clothes with you. It **may/might** snow. OR **Maybe it will** snow.
11. When the baby went to the doctor last week, she **had to have** several shots.
12. It's very cool in here. Please ~~you~~ turn up the heat. OR **Would/Could/Will/Can you** please turn up the heat?
13. You had better ~~to~~ call us before you come over. We're often away during the day.
14. The children would rather ~~to~~ see the circus than a baseball game.
15. It's such a gorgeous day. Why **don't we** go to a park or the beach?

◇ PRACTICE 28, p. 150.

(1) may . . . is . . . can . . . can
(2) should . . . can . . . should . . . should not . . . is . . . Will
(3) do not have to . . . do not have to . . . can
(4) have to . . . cannot . . . must . . . do . . . is . . . can . . . should
(5) ought to . . . prepare
(6) are . . . might . . . may . . . Maybe . . . could . . . is . . . are . . . should
(7) should . . . will . . . can change . . . should . . . should . . . should
(8) is . . . should

NOTES

NOTES

NOTES

NOTES

NOTES

NOTES

NOTES